❧

All about Flowers

❧

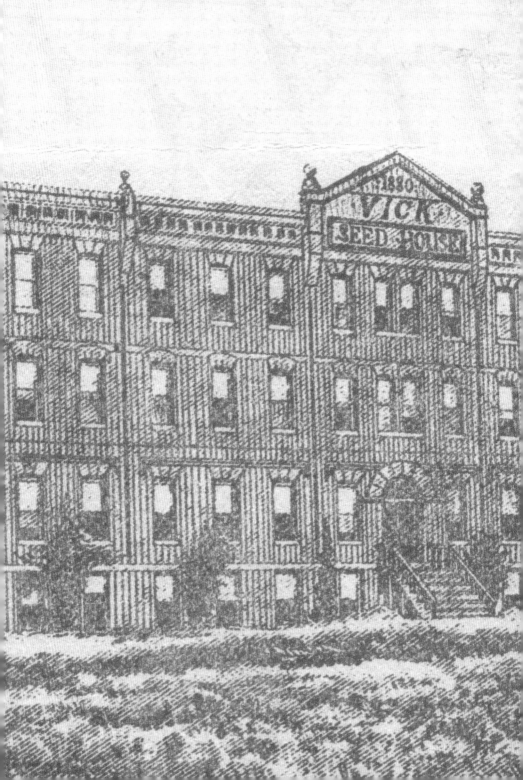

All about Flowers

James Vick's Nineteenth-Century Seed Company

THOMAS J. MICKEY

Foreword by CHARLES A. BIRNBAUM

Swallow Press / Ohio University Press ❧ Athens

Swallow Press
An imprint of Ohio University Press, Athens, Ohio 45701
ohioswallow.com

To obtain permission to quote, reprint, or otherwise reproduce or distribute material from Swallow Press / Ohio University Press publications, please contact our rights and permissions department at (740) 593-1154 or (740) 593-4536 (fax).

Printed in the United States of America
Swallow Press / Ohio University Press books are printed on acid-free paper ⊗ ™

30 29 28 27 26 25 24 23 22 21   5 4 3 2 1

Library of Congress Cataloging-in-Publication Data
Names: Mickey, Thomas J., author. | Birnbaum, Charles A., writer of foreword.
Title: All about flowers : James Vick's nineteenth-century seed company / Thomas J. Mickey, Charles A. Birnbaum.
Description: Athens, Ohio : Swallow Press, [2021] | Includes bibliographical references and index.
Identifiers: LCCN 2020020325 | ISBN 9780804012294 (trade paperback) | ISBN 9780804041140 (pdf)
Subjects: LCSH: Vick, James, 1818–1882. | Vick Seed Company. | Flowers—Marketing. | Flowers—Varieties—Seeds. | Seed industry and trade—United States. | United States—History—19th century.
Classification: LCC SB443.3 .M535 2020 | DDC 338.1/759—dc23
LC record available at https://lccn.loc.gov/2020020325

publication supported by a grant from

The Community Foundation
for
Greater New Haven

as part of the Urban Haven Project

Contents

✿   ✿

Illustrations

Foreword

❧ ❧

James Vick (1818–82) was born three years after Andrew Jackson Downing (1815–52) and three years before Frederick Law Olmsted Sr. (1822–1903). Unlike these two enormously influential tastemakers who did so much to shape both the private and shared landscapes of nineteenth-century America, Vick's name is not commonly known in landscape architecture and horticultural circles today.

Vick, like both Downing and Olmsted, began his career in publishing—first as a newspaper and magazine writer, then, beginning in 1850, as editor of the *Genesee Farmer*. In 1846, Downing, a well-published author, launched *The Horticulturist, and Journal of Rural Art and Rural Taste,* a monthly magazine for the affluent middle class. In 1852, Olmsted published *Walks and Talks of an American Farmer in England,* his first book, chronicling his travels through the slaveholding South as a *New York Times* reporter.

Downing's unexpected death in 1852 changed everything. In 1853, Vick purchased the *Horticulturist* and placed Patrick Barry (1816–90), a fellow resident of Rochester, New York, and horticulturist and nursery owner, at the helm as editor. Olmsted's career in journalism and publishing also advanced; he served as managing editor of *Putnam's Monthly Magazine* from 1855 to 1857. In March 1858, Olmsted and Calvert Vaux won the Central Park design competition.

We all know what happens next for Olmsted. Can we say the same for the entrepreneurial Vick, who in his two decades of publishing a seed catalog before adding a magazine brought Downing's domestic ideals to a broad middle-class populace?

Landscape historian David Schuyler, who has written extensively about both Downing and Vaux, suggests that for Downing wisdom was "knowledge put into action."[1] Downing's death positioned Olmsted to design the great New York City park. For others, like Vick, it fueled an attitude that, if the American landscape was to be afforded thoughtful stewardship—from rural to urban and from private to public—then there was a call to teach people how to see it.

Vick's accomplishments as a horticulturist (crossbreeding flowers such as white-double phlox), seedsman (he was among the first in the United States to import rare seeds from Europe), nursery owner (his show gardens were a regional travel destination), publisher (*Vick's Illustrated Monthly* set a standard for horticultural writing), and author are well chronicled by Thomas Mickey in this illuminating book.

Among so many other aspects of the man, we learn that Vick was a communication and marketing master. Mickey notes that by 1872, the Vick Seed Company sent out more than two hundred thousand illustrated catalogs each year, while "the total advertising bill in December 1870 amounted to $15,000," approximately $270,000 in current dollars. Vick told customers that "anyone desiring goods in this line cannot do better than send 10 cents for the Floral Guide" and that they could "deduct the 10 cents from the first order sent for seeds." That is, Vick was pioneering direct marketing before Montgomery Ward, Sears, and L.L. Bean. He also saturated the market: in 1870, when the US population was 38.5 million, one out of every 192 people received a Vick's catalog. All this in an age before the appearance of shelter magazines like *Martha Stewart Living* and *Veranda,* or HGTV with its 61 million viewers.

The marketing paid off. *Manufacturer and Builder,* a monthly which described itself as "a practical journal of industrial progress," was unwavering in its praise for *Vick's Floral Guide.* The inaugural issue (January 1869) included a glowing review: "No house can be considered complete unless the grounds surrounding it are ornamented with those choicest of decoration, flowers. Mr. Vick's pamphlet tells us not only what to do, but how to do it; and as he is a well-known authority in regard to horticultural matters, those who consult his little work can hardly avoid all serious errors."[2] Another review by the same magazine in the 1880s was equally laudatory: "Here it is again, brighter and better than ever . . . filled with just such information as is required by the gardener, the farmer, those growing plants, and everyone needing seeds or plants."[3] An 1894 review said the *Guide* "contains descriptions that describe, not mislead; illustrations that instruct, not exaggerate."[4] The journal was steadfast in its support of Vick's efforts to spread the love of floriculture for the home landscape until it ceased publication in 1897.

As Mickey notes, Vick believed that by beautifying a home and taking care of your own property, you also helped the nation. In Liberty Hyde Bailey's classic *Cyclopedia of American Horticulture,* there is a scant one-paragraph entry on James Vick. Entry author Wilhelm Miller wrote, "Vick's personality was thoroughly amiable, and his letters in 'Vick's Magazine' to children and to garden-lovers everywhere show the great hold he had on the hearts of the people."[5]

Mickey's book does much to contextualize James Vick and his seed company, whose expansive reach educated hundreds of thousands in nineteenth-century America. Revisiting his varied subjects today—from asters to zinnias and from laying out grounds to improving homes—it is not a leap to see that these ideas translate to today, a testament to what a great messenger he was.

Charles A. Birnbaum, FASLA, FAAR
Founder and President
The Cultural Landscape Foundation
Washington, DC

Acknowledgments

Many people have supported me in writing this book. Without their help you would not be reading it.

Thanks to Bridgewater State University in Bridgewater, Massachusetts, for the Faculty and Librarian Research Grant that I received from the Center for the Advancement of Research and Scholarship. The BSU Grants and Sponsored Projects Office, so ably run by Frances Jeffries, was an unending resource for grant research and writing and provided great advice on working with archival material.

I first encountered James Vick at the Harvard University Landscape Institute, where landscape art historian Elizabeth Eustis introduced me to the cultural significance of garden images in nineteenth-century garden catalogs, books, and magazines. I am also grateful to John Furlong, former director of the Landscape Institute, who encouraged me to write this book and make James Vick's ideas on gardening more available to the general public.

Special thanks to our longtime Rochester, New York, friends Mary Ann and Carey O'Neill. Though Carey has now passed on, I am grateful for their hospitality. I often stayed at their home while researching Vick in various archives in the city. Sometimes the dinner conversation would even turn to Mr. Vick, the city's famous nineteenth-century seed merchant.

Various collections of Vick's catalogs and monthly magazine were made available to me, including the James Vick Seed Company collection of seed catalogs at the University of Delaware Special Collections in Newark, Delaware, and the *Vick's Illustrated Monthly* collection at the Five College Library Depository at the University of Massachusetts Amherst. The following institutions in Rochester were helpful in locating other important primary and secondary materials on Vick: the Rochester Public Library, Strong Museum, Rochester Museum and Science Center, Rochester Historical Society, Rochester Civic Garden Center, University of Rochester Rare Book Collection, and Rochester Institute of Technology.

Thanks to Kirk Hazlett, Kirsten Whitten, Geraldine Laufer, and Beth Cody for reading an earlier version of the book and offering helpful suggestions.

I am grateful to Karen Bussolini and Christine Froehlich, who, on separate occasions, both told me about present-day Vick descendants.

I must give a special note of thanks to James Vick's two great-great-grandsons, James and Jonathan Vick, and Jonathan's daughter Cecilia Lyon Staunton. They graciously offered me access to their personal collection of original Vick Seed Company publications and illustrations.

The former head of digital library services at Bridgewater State University, Ellen Dubinsky, and her successor Xiaocan (Lucy) Wang kindly scanned most of the wonderful illustrations you will see in the pages to come.

Ohio University Press believed in this book from the beginning and encouraged me to write it. I am so proud to be associated with OUP.

Finally, thanks to my wife, Rita Mae, who supported me in so many ways throughout the research and writing of this book.

Introduction

❧ ❧

customer wrote to Rochester, New York, seedsman James Vick in 1879, stating, "I must say one word for your *Monthly Magazine.* I like it very much, as it is all about flowers, and that is just what I like."[1] Vick's own words about the love of flowers both motivated him and at the same time inspired his customers, who became instrumental in building a business that would spread from coast to coast.

Once, while visiting Rochester, I stopped to browse in a used bookstore. I mentioned to the owner that I planned to write a book about seedsman James Vick. He said to me, "That's a good idea. It's funny there's no book on him."

That chance visit told me Vick belonged to the city's history. Many people in Rochester know that Vick ran a successful seed business in the nineteenth century, but I wonder, how many know that his goal as a seed company owner was to spread the love of flowers?

This book came about because I wanted to tell the story of Vick and his business. In newspaper articles of that period I found many references to his seed company as the "biggest in the world," "known across the country," and a "purveyor of quality seeds." After I read his seed catalogs and the early volumes of his magazine that he edited, I saw what made his company so successful. It was his bond with his customers. He treated them as essential in his business, and they felt that respect, as is clear in the many letters he received from them.

꽃

What follows is the story of a man whose personal and passionate approach to his business and his customers changed the cultural face of his nation in ways that are felt even now, over a century and a half after Vick's prime. His pioneering approach to marketing along with his personal commitment to gardening shaped the gardening business of the present, from the style of modern garden writing to the choice of plants popular in gardens today.

Vick's story begins in the early nineteenth century. To understand his accomplishments, we will take a look at how people of the time learned about the garden, its plants, and what the garden should look like.

If you were wealthy, you could travel the world to visit gardens. You could read the latest books and journals about horticulture. You might even join a plant group like the Massachusetts Horticultural Society, where like-minded people, mostly men, would discuss their greenhouses, landscapes, and plants, especially their fruit trees.

If you were middle class, perhaps you joined a botany club that banded together in a shared interest in the science of plants. The seed and nursery catalog would have been your primary link to what was new in gardening. By the second half of the nineteenth century, the seed catalog that arrived in the mail had become more than simply a listing of seeds or plants for sale. The catalog would include essays, descriptions of plants, advice on how to care for them, and illustrations. When Vick began his seed company in 1861, the world was already familiar with the seed catalog, expecting it both to offer new plants and to teach something about gardening.

In part thanks to Vick's efforts, by the middle of the nineteenth century, Rochester had become a site of intense activity in the seed and nursery industries, earning it the nickname "Flower City." Seed and plant businesses appealed to the middle class, who sought lawns, trees, shrubs, and flower beds for the home landscape.

Flowers became an important garden focus for the country during the second half of the nineteenth century. Their color brightened up both the garden and the rooms of the house. Flowers also acquired meanings as symbols of religious faith, morality, civic duty, and even of blessings from God. Vick often used such themes to motivate gardeners, seeking to spread the love of floriculture.

The horticultural historian Denise Wiles Adams examined the seed and nursery catalogs of this period in the course of research for her extensive study of American garden plants. She writes, "Victorian gardens in California resembled gardens of that era in the East, with emphasis on strategic placement of trees and curvilinear paths in the Downingesque mode, as well as implementation of the gaudy ribbon bedding style of brightly colored annuals."[2] By 1900, flowers filled the gardens of both laborers and the middle class in cities and towns across the country, planted in beds, borders, and containers, thanks in part to Mr. Vick.

Vick's early writing and editing experience prepared him well. Before starting his seed business, he had written for and edited several garden publications in the Rochester area. He had the ability to put vividly into words his ideas about gardening and, of course, about flowers. That skill served him when it came time to write his own seed catalog and, in 1878, to publish his own garden magazine, *Vick's Illustrated Monthly.*

Vick published his magazine under four different titles during the four years he edited it. For the sake of simplicity, I will refer to the magazine throughout this book, including in the notes, as *Vick's Illustrated Monthly*—the title he chose for his first issue, published in January 1878. Entries in the bibliography provide information on the titles he used for specific issues.

Over the twenty years that Vick managed his seed business, it grew from a small operation located in his attic to fill a four-story red brick building that housed the various departments that made up his company. The need for expanded physical space indicates not only his success but also the importance of the company to the city of Rochester.

Vick promoted his business in various ways, including maintaining a show garden at both his home and his trial farm located outside the city. These allowed his customers to see hundreds of the flowers he sold in his catalog. He also exhibited his flowers at state fairs around the country.

Through his writing and devoted service to his customers, he sold the love of flowers along with flower seeds. His customers in their letters would often attest to loving flowers and even to living a fuller life because of Vick's words and his precious seeds. In 1881, a reader from Massachusetts wrote that "there is no deception in the language of flowers. They are not necessary to our lower, material life, and, just for this reason, they speak unmistakable [*sic*] of the love of their unseen Creator. There is much that is hard and productive of sorrow in this sin-plagued world of ours; and, had we no flowers, I believe existence would be hard to be borne."[3]

Vick instructed his customers on how to grow their flowers in beds, borders, or containers. He gave detailed information on laying out the garden and the proper way to display flowers in a vase that would sit on the lawn. He regularly suggested certain flowers as an essential part of any bed, border, or garden vase. To this day, his recommendations inform garden choices. He became the voice of flowers to Victorian America, and we still love and grow many of the flowers Vick popularized.

Flowers were essential in Victorian America not only because they were flowers, but because entrepreneurial people like James Vick *told* customers that flowers ought to be a part of life and that they would add love and beauty to daily existence.

Vick's efforts to reach his audience and sell them seeds might seem a simple process. Not at all. Vick demonstrated innovation and creative genius in his ability to enlist his readers to become his customers. His relationship with his customers became an early example of the power of marketing that is both honest and personal.

Today, Vick's marketing skill might well be recognized as what marketing specialist Robyn Blakeman calls "integrated marketing communication." As she puts it, the person who will buy the product needs to see "what's in it for me?"[4] James Vick understood that.

Integrated marketing communication looks for answers to three questions: What needs to be accomplished in selling the product? Who is the target audience? What is the motivation?[5] Vick proposed from the beginning that a home was not complete without a bed of colorful flowers. He knew that since it was likely to be the woman of the household who would both buy his seeds and plant the garden, he needed to enlist her in his business. Thus, in the process of seeking to spread beauty around the country one garden at a time, women became his primary market and simultaneously helped him build the company.

Vick was not only a skillful marketer but also one who genuinely viewed his customers as more than purchasers of seeds. He saw them as his fellow gardeners and his friends. In the process of building his company, James Vick became the personality behind the Vick seed packet, projecting an image of trust and creating a product that was both recognizable and dependable.

James Vick built his company before words like image, brand, target audience, and communication strategy entered the business vocabulary. Though he may not have known the words, he put what they meant into practice.

You will see in the following pages several of the original chromolithographs of flowers from both Vick's seed catalog and his magazine. They shine today as brightly as they did when Vick first chose to include them, giving insight to the allure Vick held for his customers. His passion and his incredible business sense combined to shape gardening culture, then and to this day.

1

❧ ❧

Vick the Writer

ames Vick *wrote* his seed business into existence. His words don't just tell his story. They *are* his story.

From the beginning, Vick was a writer, and he sharpened his skills throughout his life. When he wrote articles or answered letters from his customers, he chose his words well, always intent on being understood clearly and on building a community of gardeners who loved flowers. Long before he began writing his own catalog in the early 1860s and his magazine in the 1870s, he had been involved in publishing for many years.

In 1833, at the age of fifteen, James Vick sailed to America with his parents from Portsmouth, England. Arriving in New York, he set out to learn the printer's trade. He set type on various publications, including a new magazine called the *Knickerbocker,* where he met journalist (and later politician and reformer) Horace Greeley. The *Knickerbocker* was a monthly literary publication appealing to the educated reader who cared about politics as well the arts. Greeley, a few years older than Vick, had arrived in New York in 1831 with the dream of becoming an editor and publisher. After leaving the *Knickerbocker* in 1834, he went on to found a weekly literary and news magazine called the *New-Yorker*.

When Vick moved to Rochester in 1837, he continued to work in the publishing business, starting by setting type for several newspapers. He soon rose to become the first foreman of Frederick Douglass's newspaper, the *North Star*. Strongly reflecting the abolitionist ideals of his mentor, Horace Greeley, Vick managed the publication in which Douglass denounced slavery and advocated for freedom for all.[1]

❧

But the country's diverse readers were interested in more than politics. From the early 1800s, farm-related journals, some weekly and others monthly, were published in many cities and towns. Though the names of such publications might include the words "horticulture" or "garden," these "papers," as they were generally called, were written for farmers needing to keep up to date on the newest methods and materials for producing agricultural crops. Sometimes, though, they did include articles for readers interested in horticulture or even ads specifically targeting the gardener.

In 1831, Rochester publisher Luther Tucker had the former group of readers in mind when he founded his *Genesee Farmer*, a journal of agricultural improvement and reform.[2] Also in Rochester, beginning in 1850, Daniel D. T. Moore, with an "able corps of Assistants and Contributors," published *Moore's Rural New Yorker*, a weekly that included articles on both farming and gardening.

In this active publishing environment, James Vick found his niche. He wrote and edited several of these journals and ultimately began his own. From 1849 to 1855, Vick served as both writer and editor for the *Genesee Farmer*. In 1849, he also became corresponding secretary of the Monroe County Agricultural Society and in that group met many of the key figures in the agricultural and horticultural business in the Rochester area.

After the sudden death in 1852 of Andrew Jackson Downing, the most famous American landscape gardener of that time, Vick purchased Downing's magazine, the *Horticulturist*. He asked his friend Patrick Barry, from

Rochester's well-known and respected Ellwanger and Barry Nursery, to assume the job of editor. After just one year, because he did not have a nursery of his own to fund the magazine, Vick had to sell it, admitting his own lack of preparation and forethought. He would later correct the mistake, combining his writing career with a new one in seed sales, but not before he gained considerably more experience as a writer and editor.

In 1855, he bought the venerable *Genesee Farmer*. Under his ownership, the writing improved and the emphasis shifted toward horticulture and away from general farming. Vick added a section called the Horticultural Department, edited by Joseph Frost. A year later he sold the journal to seedsman and nursery owner Joseph Harris, who also served as editor. By 1860, the name of the publication had changed to *The Genesee Farmer: A Monthly Journal Devoted to Agriculture & Horticulture, Domestic and Rural Economy,* which Harris described in his Editor's Notes as "an indispensable companion to every tiller of the soil, whether he cultivates much or little land."[3]

From 1856 to 1857, Vick published his own garden magazine, the *Rural Annual and Horticultural Directory.* In volume 1, in a column titled "The Lawn and the Flower Garden," he wrote, "In order to make our work complete and interesting to all classes of horticultural readers, a few hints on the arrangement and management of the Flower Garden appear desirable."[4] Vick encouraged Irish-born landscape gardener Robert Robinson Scott (1827–77) to write the section dedicated to the flower garden, and he became a frequent contributor.

While Vick was developing his publishing skills, he also gained substantial knowledge of agriculture as both business and hobby, came to know many professionals and amateurs in farming and gardening, and deepened his understanding of what growers needed and loved. His later expansion into the seed trade drew on his knowledge not only of the practicalities of business but of the entire culture that supported seed sales in the United States.

From 1857 to 1862, while Vick was the horticultural editor of *Moore's Rural New Yorker,* he was experimenting with seeds in his spare time.[5] In 1860, he began his seed business, and a year later he published his first catalog, the *Floral Guide and Illustrated Catalogue,* the name that he would use for the next two decades. At first he wrote his seed catalog twice a year, for the spring and late

fall. Later, he published it four times a year. He let his readers know that the illustrations were prepared from plants in his own garden and often mentioned
that his artist was busy at work on the material for a coming issue. Vick knew
that gardens growing from his seeds were the best way of promoting business:
"The gardens of my customers are the best advertisements I have."[6]

❧

At the same time that ornamental plantings were appearing in the pleasure
gardens of wealthy Americans, middle-class and working-class families
were also growing flowers. As the *Eagle Country Press* of Polo, Illinois, published in 1867, "All who spend a few dollars in beautifying their grounds
with flowers will find a rich reward in the enjoyment of the beauty thus
added to their homes."[7] The interest in flower growing that was spreading
around the country was due in no small part to the commercial seed catalogs. Companies selling flower seeds multiplied after 1850, and many tar-
geted specifically those middle-class and working families.

In his introduction to the Lawn and Flower Garden section of the *Rural
and Horticultural Directory* in 1856, Vick had written, "More has been done
to enrich the conservatories of the more wealthy of our citizens by foreign
rare introductions than to extend the general taste for gardening among the
operative [i.e., working] classes." In the same issue he stated his life-long
goal: "We hope to see every family in possession of a flower garden."[8]

To accomplish this, Vick wanted to help his readers become more
knowledgeable about gardening and to make gardening, especially with
flowers, available to all classes of people. He wrote, "So long as the taste [for
gardening] is confined to a few, or at least the means for gratifying that
taste, just so long will we continue dependent on the more perfect arrangements of Europe for our supplies, not only of new plants and new fruits, but
for the current horticultural literature."[9]

By the late 1860s, many of Vick's customers were so enthusiastic that
they began asking for a photograph of him. Finally, in the 1872 edition of his
seed catalog, which he sent to a hundred and fifty thousand customers, he
included a photo of himself (fig. 1.1). Those less fortunate had to be satisfied

with a lithograph portrait. He wrote, "So many persons ask for my Photograph during the busy season, when it is very difficult to furnish them, that I determined to present all my own customers, if not all, with a copy."[10]

Almost as a prelude to the magazine he would start in 1878, Vick wrote in his catalog of 1873, "We have long felt the need of more frequent communication with our customers, and this was the object mainly in making our Guide [catalog] quarterly. Could we spare the time from other duties, nothing would please us more than to visit our friends Monthly with a little counsel, a little information, and a good deal of gossip. In time we may be able to accomplish this."[11]

Only after he had managed his seed business for several years did Vick take his next and greatest step in writing. The first volume of *Vick's Illustrated Monthly* appeared in January 1878. In the years leading up to this new venture he'd developed a name and a company, ensuring an audience ready to support his magazine—unlike his earlier, doomed efforts with the *Horticulturist.*

He published *Vick's Illustrated Monthly* in order to have the space to write in more detail about plants and their cultivation, to cover a given topic in greater particularity in each issue. He would also be able to answer questions about garden problems, such as why a reader's plant didn't grow or why insects seemed to be invading a particular flower.

Each issue of the magazine contained articles, woodcut illustrations, and often a colored plate in the front "painted expressly for Vick's Monthly Magazine" (fig. 1.2). Vick said of the magazine, "It is designed to spread a taste for the beautiful all over the land, and to encourage the culture of Flowers by insuring success, as much as it is possible to do so, by printed instructions."[12] Vick himself supplied many of the articles, which he wrote in a friendly tone. He also included items by correspondents as well as letters from his readers, which he often answered.

Vick had proved already that his writing could touch his customers. In the process, he became a spokesperson for Victorian floriculture. In the first issue of the magazine, Vick wrote, "Each number of the Monthly will contain thirty-two pages, printed on the best paper we can procure, and

liberally illustrated with engravings, while with every issue we shall give an elegant colored plate of some flower, or family of flowers, as fine and true to nature as the work of the best artists and our own supervision can produce."[13] In fact, it would be recognized in a 1901 tribute to Vick that *Vick's Illustrated Monthly* "was the best illustrated magazine of floriculture that America had in the late seventies and early eighties."[14]

His readers responded well. One customer, whose signature was simply "A Lover of Flowers," wrote, "We pity the person who has acres of land, but yet can find no room for flowers—who sees nothing beautiful about him except that which puts a dollar in his pocket, and who brings up his children in the same sordid manner."[15]

Vick's readers appreciated his descriptions of flowers, along with his encouragement to plant and discuss them. One reader wrote, "Mr. Vick, I never take up one of your Magazines but it sets me quite in a flutter, and I feel as if I were a full member of a talking club, whose sole duty is to talk flowers." In the same issue, another reader said, "A love for flowers does not make us rich, in the common idea of riches, but there has never been, nor ever will be, any money made that will buy the pleasure that a love and knowledge of flowers brings."[16]

Vick wrote during the high Victorian period in America, and he encouraged a Victorian style of gardening that focused on colorful flowers, whether annuals, bulbs, or perennials. One reader wrote to Vick saying, "History will yet tell what you have done by cultivating a taste for flowers in Republican America."[17]

Vick said, "We design to make everything very plain and give instructions that all can understand."[18] A customer from Arkansas described the magazine as a chance to form a relationship with "Mr. Vick," saying, "You now have a most suitable medium for your subscribers to exchange the fruits of experience and sentiments on gardening, and they ought to avail themselves of the opportunity."[19]

In later years, Vick sometimes wrote about the origin of his career. In 1878 he recalled, "There were plenty of good florists and cultivators of flowers and horticultural writers before we planted a seed or admired a flower, or wrote a line; yet we thought that the taste for flowers was making too little progress, that the writings of the day were not always adapted to the wants of the people, and, perhaps, with some presumption, believed that we could say a good many simple things that would at once interest and instruct. So we commenced writing and publishing, and importing and growing flowers and seeds."[20]

Vick began his magazine as a writer and seed merchant interested in spreading the love of flowers throughout the country. The language in his articles and letters reveals his goals. He wrote to relate to his customers, and in the process, he sold them flower seeds. He was building a community of gardeners through his writing, and that writing built the company and Vick's reputation.

✷ *Figure 1.2.* Phlox and pansy. (*Vick's Illustrated Monthly,* 1878.)

2

Flowers in the Garden

Flora, Goddess of Flowers

We often use the Latin term *flora* when speaking about plants or flowers, but the name also refers to Flora, the Roman goddess of plants.

Titus Tatius, who ruled with Romulus, is said to have introduced her cult to Rome. Flora's duties were to provide the blooms to flowering plants so they would thrive, grow, and reproduce and to stand as their champion against drought and other disasters. Flora's temple in Rome stood near the Circus Maximus, and her festival, Floralia, was instituted in 238 BC. The celebration included floral wreaths worn in the hair, much as by modern participants in May Day celebrations.

In 1731, Sir John Clerk of Pennycuik wrote a poem called "The Country Seat" about the gardens and estates of England. In the poem he said, "Where

Flora with a Knot of gaudy Flowrs [*sic*] / may dress her lovely head."[1] To understand the reference, it helps to look at a bit of Roman history. A representation of Flora's head, distinguished by a floral crown, appeared on coins of the Roman Republic. In paintings of Flora since that time, such a crown has been an essential element.

The wealthy in eighteenth-century England, who had adopted a new, naturalistic landscape design for what they considered the "modern" garden, also developed a love of all things classical Greek and Roman, including horticulture and agriculture. English landscape gardener Batty Langley, in his important book on landscape design, *New Principles of Gardening* (1728), wrote that the landscape should include "a Flower-Garden, enrich'd with the most fragrant Flowers and beautiful Statues," in particular a depiction of Flora.[2]

Landowner Henry Hoare's showplace, Stourhead, west of London, included not only the statue but a temple as well, built in 1745 by landscape gardener and architect Henry Flitcroft. The *London Chronicle* wrote of this temple in 1757, "Here is the figure of the Goddess (i.e. a Ceres or Flora), with her proper emblems, standing in front of you as you open the door."[3] Hoare's temple stands today, and over its entrance a Latin inscription still reads, "Keep away, anyone profane, keep away." Hoare wanted any visitor to enter his garden in the right spirit.

American seed company owner George Thorburn also recognized the role of Flora in providing the flowers that mark the good taste of the homeowner, "from the humblest cottage enclosure to the most extensive park and grounds." He joined others in invoking the figure of Flora, when in 1838 he quoted an earlier article from the *Journal of Health:* "A neglected, weed-grown garden, or its total absence, marks the indolence and unhappy state of those who have been thus neglectful of Flora's favours."[4]

James Vick, too, promoted Flora's spirit in the landscape. He even named a chromolithograph in his magazine *Flora's Jewels* (fig. 2.1).

❧

The key element in landscape gardening is variety. Even more than concepts such as "natural," "informal," or "wild," even more than the symbolic content

of the design, variety emerged as the most important structural element of the eighteenth-century English landscape garden.[5] This element of variety included the planting of flowers, especially in the parterre area. "Parterre" refers to a geometric arrangement of beds of plants like boxwood separated by a series of walks or grassed areas. William Shenstone—whose estate "the Leasowes" was considered the preeminent example of the modern landscape garden of the time—divided gardening into three types: kitchen gardening, parterre gardening, and "landskip" or picturesque gardening.[6]

❧❦

Flowers took on various meanings important at a particular time and place. Flowers in the late-Victorian nineteenth century, for example, represented a link to civility, to community, to morality, to God, all wrapped up in a plant and its flower. Vick sought to encourage gardening with flowers as a way to offer contact with nature, but also to set a moral tone for the home environment of the gardener.

Today, flowers are important for reasons that each gardener might explain in a different way. Some love that they bring color to an otherwise dull setting. The colors also vary depending on the plant variety. Perhaps a gardener chooses only one color for a garden, like the white garden at England's Sissinghurst Castle or the blue and white garden at Sonnenberg Gardens and Mansion in upstate New York. The color of a flower may bring back memories from childhood gardening with a parent or grandparent. The yellow of the black-eyed Susan reminds one gardener I know of the happy times spent with her mother working in the garden.

That there are so many colors to choose from amazes. The shades of blue could range from very light to a dark, almost purple blue. In a clematis flower you can find a light blue like 'Ramona' and then a darker blue like 'Perle d'Azur.' Not only can a gardener choose a particular color for a flower, but often within that variety there may be lighter or darker versions. One reason to visit flower gardens is to see what other people are planting and learn the

Figure 2.1. Chromo E. *Flora's Jewels*. Statuette of Flora holding thirty-seven varieties of flowers. (*Vick's Floral Guide*, 1874.)

possibilities of color in a flower. Tulips present an array of color, and of course, in some varieties they also offer more than one color on a flower.

The imagery around the garden has long fascinated artists, including writers. We even call "Paradise" a garden. Poets have always been delighted with the beauties of a garden.[7] They have often proclaimed the glory of flowers. Shakespeare used flowers to express feeling and emotions in the characters of his plays.[8]

Today we use flowers to show feelings of both joy and sorrow. At weddings and other special occasions, like the birth of a new baby in the family, flowers take center stage. The colors are usually light in tone. Flowers also appear at funerals, but often in darker tones to symbolize the darkness of the passing of a loved one.

In both nineteenth-century Europe and America, there was much interest in the language of flowers, which went by the name of "floriography." A rose meant love. The jonquil meant "I desire a return of affection."[9] Each flower defined a feeling or sensation, and people used them to convey that emotional state. An artfully arranged bouquet could be a complete letter. One writer informs us that "between 1827 and 1923, there were at least 98 different flower dictionaries in circulation in the United States."[10]

❧

Not long ago, Boston's Arnold Arboretum announced that it was sending members of its staff to search for plants both in the United States and abroad. Following a year of planning, eight collectors would be in the field, pursuing scores of target species—just as with many other such quests before and since sponsored by the Arboretum.[11] Other public gardens, like Philadelphia's Longwood Gardens, undertake similar excursions to seek out plants around the world, including trees, shrubs, perennials, and annuals. Many new hydrangea shrubs, for example, have come to the United States from such hunting in gardens around the world. Such hunts ultimately provide the gardener with new plant choices, including new kinds of flowers.

Plant hunting has long been a way for gardeners to enjoy plants that come from other parts of the world. In the sixteenth century, England's

Hatfield House supported John Tradescant the Elder (1570–1638) in his search for plants in other countries. Since then, but especially in the nineteenth century, England has introduced hundreds of new plants, like the South African *pelargonium*, or geranium. Most of them came from Asia, Africa, and the Americas. Thanks to a healthy nursery trade in both common and exotic plants, these same plant varieties soon came to American gardens as well.

Such novel flower specimens became important in the garden, simply because they were different and new. Those two words will continue to distinguish a plant for generations as the key motivating factor in flower choice for the garden. Often the seed and nursery catalogs promoted a flower simply because it was new or at least unknown to the ordinary middle-class or cottage gardener.

Seed merchants also played a role in determining flower selection by their customers. For instance, James Vick offered his favorite annuals for sale, and customers in turn chose their own favorites from that group. One wrote a poem on her twelve favorite annuals, all offered in the pages of Vick's catalog, and Vick included the poem in his magazine.

❧

The farmer was always on the search for seed that would provide the highest profit from his labor. By the mid-nineteenth century, hybridized seeds for crops like corn, barley, and rice presented farmers with better yields. This happened all over the world, including Europe and the United States, where a young nation was intent on feeding its ever-growing population.

Farmers would display their new grain and vegetable products at fairs, where other farmers would learn about the seeds that had produced such bounty. When a new variety of a plant offered important qualities like better size, color, taste, and disease resistance, farmers were quick to try that new seed.

The same was true in the flower seed industry. As Vick wrote, "Every year seedlings are produced and named which are considered as surpassing their predecessors in some point of excellence."[12] A better petunia, a stronger pansy, or a verbena with bigger flowers were all possible with hybridizing. By the late nineteenth century, commercial seedsmen were quite important in the spread of these many new vegetable and flower varieties.[13] In 1833, for example, Phila-delphia nurseryman Robert Buist exhibited thirty-seven varieties of dahlia at the Pennsylvania Horticultural Society's annual exhibition. In 1844, nursery-man Charles Mason Hovey of Cambridge, Massachusetts, offered 160 variet-ies of the dahlia in his catalog. And by 1873, James Vick was cultivating five acres of dahlias in Rochester. In 1878, Vick said, "The *Dahlia* is our best au-tumn flower. We can depend upon it until frost, no matter how long de-layed."[14] Vick made available to his customers dozens of dahlia varieties, most of them the result of hybridizing (fig. 2.2). His praise of a particular plant might be read by a gardener in some far western state like Illinois or Missouri and thereby spread the popularity of that variety to a wider populace.

One nineteenth-century dahlia, 'White Queen,' achieved a reputation as a most desirable plant in the garden. In 1883, the English publication *Gardening Illustrated* called it "the finest white Dahlia in existence—perfec-tion, in fact, in every respect."[15] Another English garden magazine wrote, "Nothing can surpass it either for planting in large masses on lawns or as an autumn bedding plant for large spaces, more especially in parks."[16] Vick recommended this dahlia in his garden magazine as well.

Another white dahlia, 'White Aster,' appeared in 1879 and is still on the market today. Some say it is the oldest dahlia variety still grown. In the nineteenth century, different varieties of dahlia were often planted with one another in the trial garden, resulting in the appearance of new colors and sizes of blossom. The outcome was a rich selection, and hundreds of new dahlias appeared on the market due to such crossing of varieties. It was impossible to keep up with the new cultivars available to a gardener. In 1895, Jacob Alexander from East Bridgewater, Massachusetts—or "the dahlia king," as he referred to himself—grew an immense variety.

Breeding of new plants in a scientific manner, however, did not begin in earnest until the beginning of the twentieth century. At that time, Cornell horticulturist Liberty Hyde Bailey, a prolific writer and early leader in horti-cultural education in the United States, inaugurated formal plant breeding.[17]

ॐ

ॐ *Figure 2.2.* Dahlias. (*Vick's Monthly Magazine*, 1878.)

Perhaps it is our need for change that drives a gardener to try new plants. Sometimes they work just fine, and other times you wonder why you bothered to plant them at all. Today, catalogs from seed companies or nurseries are important sources for learning about change in flower choices, but of course their true business is to tempt the consumer with new and better plants.

New hybrids afford growers the opportunity to present novel choices to the home garden market. It is not unusual for such new varieties to spend several years in a trial period to make sure that the plants will perform in the garden. Thus, a grower might send out dozens of samples of a new plant to select gardeners to try for a year or two before it comes on the market, if it does at all.

❧

At the same time, however, gardeners continue to plant many of the same flowers every year, just out of habit. Gardeners get used to planting certain varieties in the flower bed, and those varieties remain their choice season after season.

On a trip to a garden center or box store in May to purchase bedding plants, you see the same varieties from the previous year. The store carries the same varieties because the owner understands the importance of recognition on the part of the customer and therefore knows what will sell. Both are dealing with a familiar product.

It is in looking at the plant as a product that we begin to understand why the home gardener of today may display such a limited palette. Today there are two hundred varieties of the perennial *Heuchera*. Who needs that many? A garden center will choose a few that are already familiar to the gardener and perhaps one new variety. It is no surprise that the choice becomes defined for the gardener rather than by the gardener.

❧

A number of factors drove the growth in sales of flower seeds in the second half of the nineteenth century in America. More people around the country, whether middle class or working class, could afford to take up gardening as a hobby. Gardening by then had expanded beyond simply growing vegetables for the table to include ornamental gardening, especially with flowers,

THE QUEEN OF FLOWERS

Figure 2.3. Roses. (*Vick's Magazine*, 1882.)

which helped to fill a bit of the leisure time that people enjoyed. Though newer vegetable varieties were not ignored, gardeners wanted to plant the newest phlox, asters, and petunias in order to enjoy the colors and smells.

Modern advances in communication and transportation spurred the growth of suburbs. Gardening contributed to the social status of the suburban homeowner, whose large lot with its lawn and flower beds became an important indicator that the homeowner had "arrived."

Whether in the village, suburb, or city, people were buying seeds for the garden from businesses rather than saving their own seeds, just as they bought clothes from a clothing store rather than making their own. They bought ketchup and horseradish from Heinz rather than spending hours in the kitchen preparing such foods, as they had for decades previously. Mass production and distribution of goods for the home also made it possible for James Vick to build his new four-story company headquarters in the residential area of beautiful East Street in Rochester.

Seeds for the garden had to come from a trusted source as a guarantee that the seed would grow, and grow true to type. A gardener did not know if the seeds from this year's flowers would produce the same flower next year, so every spring the search was on for dependable seeds. Vick guaranteed them to his customers and people trusted him.

❧

Vick's message was that the gardener could contribute to the moral tone of the country simply by growing flowers. A garden, as he said, would bring the gardener that much closer to that first Garden of Eden. A customer from Kansas wrote to Vick these words of praise: "No missionary to Foreign Fields has ever done more for the common cause of Humanity."[18] From as far away as China one wrote, "I read your books with delight. You are scattering beauty around the world and brightening homes in all lands."[19]

One correspondent even brought it all back around to the goddess Flora. A Catholic nun, Sister M. Eulalia from West Virginia, wrote, "I have half a mind to say St. Vick, so kind and generous have you proved yourself, and even the Church I am sure will confirm your position at the head of the Goddess Flora's Calendar."[20]

3

❧ ❧

The Garden Industry in the Nineteenth Century

eed company and nursery owners in the nineteenth century needed to promote their products, especially to the growing middle class. By the end of the century, by which time there were a greater number of newspapers and magazines, that effort included marketing the latest in garden fashion to consumers.

Early in the century, those who had money and acres of land had ways of learning about what was popular in gardening, including the planting and care of flowers, that were inaccessible to the working and the middle classes. Some of the wealthier individuals could become gentlemen farmers because they had the resources to cultivate rows of fruit trees and to build greenhouses to nurture the newest tropical flowering plants, like orchids and camellias.

If you were wealthy you could choose to landscape your property, often a summer residence a few miles outside the city, in the English style. You could cultivate the latest varieties and, of course, have an array of green-houses for nurturing new plants, overwintering plants for the summer garden, and displaying your tropical plant collection.

꒰꒱

For example, in the early years of the nineteenth century, wealthy Bostonians could learn about trends in gardening while traveling through Europe to visit gardens like England's Stourhead and Chatsworth or France's grand garden of Versailles. They read the latest books and magazines on horticulture, mostly from England. They joined groups like the Massachusetts Horticultural Society (founded in 1829 by a few gentlemen farmers and local nurserymen) and the American Pomological Society (1848), which became a resource for fruit tree growers. These groups shared information on such issues as the newest varieties of fruit, improved methods of growing, and problems with destructive insects.

In Brookline, Massachusetts, a town just outside Boston, Colonel Thomas Handasyd Perkins (1764–1854) (fig. 3.1) cultivated such a garden on his country estate, which many considered to be the most advanced in horticultural science of any in New England.[1] The rural property with its white summerhouse sat at the corner of Warren and Heath Streets, an area that has long attracted the wealthy and powerful of Boston.

Perkins, an early member of the Massachusetts Horticultural Society, typified how prominent American men of the day chose to garden. Historians Carl Seaburg and Stanley Paterson write in their biography of Perkins that "encouragement was given to ornamental gardening, with an eye to the art of landscaping."[2] The choice reflected the latest fashion in gardening and illustrated the importance of keeping up with current tastes. The first volume of *Gardens of Colony and State,* published in 1931, mentioned the flowers at the Perkins estate: "Visitors noted in September 1835 the annual and other flowers blooming profusely."[3]

In the late eighteenth century, English landscape design had become park-like, following the no-frills look of the landscapes of Lancelot

æð *Figure 3.1.* Thomas Handasyd Perkins (1764–1854). (*The Athenaeum Centenary* [Boston: Boston Athenaeum, 1907].)

"Capability" Brown, named royal gardener by George III. Brown's signature look was a lawn that ideally swept down to woods bordering a property. Flower beds were absent. Humphry Repton (1752–1818), Brown's successor, brought flowers back into the landscape, introducing terraces of flowers around the house to bridge the gap Brown's style left between building and landscape.[4]

The archives of the Boston Athenaeum include the 1849 landscape plan for Perkins's Brookline property, which followed the Repton model that had become attractive to wealthy Americans of the early nineteenth century. It is no surprise, therefore, that the plan included flower beds, indicated by rows and rows of colorful tiny dots. Perkins's grandson, the painter and architect Edward Clarke Cabot (1818–1901), drew up the plan, which features extensive lawns, greenhouses, a kitchen garden, and orchards. Cabot is also known for designing the Athenaeum's new building (1849) at 10½ Beacon Street near the Massachusetts State House (fig. 3.2).

Perkins cultivated plants from around the world, including a grapevine from England's Sir Joseph Paxton, the head gardener at Chatsworth. Paxton, one of the most important gardeners in England, also designed the Crystal Palace for the London Great Exhibition of 1851. Boston historian Thomas G. Cary wrote in 1856 that "after his retirement from commerce, Col. Perkins found sufficient occupation in the management of his property; in various matters of a public nature which interested him; and in the cultivation of trees, and particularly of fruits and flowers, on his estate at Brookline."[5] After his visit to the Perkins property, the fruit grower and former Massachusetts Horticultural Society president Marshall Wilder wrote in 1881, "For fifty years Colonel Perkins's estate was kept in the best manner by experienced foreign gardeners, and at an expense of more than ten thousand dollars annually. He frequently received trees and plants from Europe, the products of which were prominent at the exhibitions of the Massachusetts Horticultural Society."[6]

⊱ *Figure 3.2.* Boston Athenaeum, 1855. (*The Athenaeum Centenary* [Boston: Boston Athenaeum, 1907].)

The Perkinses' daughter Eliza married Samuel Cabot Jr. Their son Lewis built another mansion on the same property in 1895, only yards from where his grandfather's white summerhouse once stood. This became known as the Cabot Estate. In 1915 the new owner, Mrs. Henry Lapham, hired the Olmsted firm, whose Brookline office was not far, to design a garden. National garden magazines featured pictures of its splendid flower borders and flower beds in bloom. The house stood until the 1990s, when it was torn down, even though it had earlier been declared a historic landmark.

If, like Colonel Perkins, you were wealthy and interested in gardening, you also had ready access to books and papers. You might read periodicals like John Claudius Loudon's *Gardener's Magazine* and Andrew Jackson Downing's *Horticulturist*. Your garden library probably would include English horticulturist Philip Miller's classic book *The Gardener's Dictionary* (which had reached its eighth edition before his death in 1771 and its ninth by 1807) and Philadelphia seedsman Bernard M'Mahon's *The American Gardener's Calendar* (1806).

By the latter half of the nineteenth century, the Massachusetts Horticultural Society had expanded its membership and gave any gardener, including those of the middle and working classes, the same opportunity to learn through annual public exhibitions and publications. The third Horticultural Hall, the society's headquarters, was built in 1901 across from Boston's Symphony Hall, where it continued its programs for all to learn about gardening and the most popular plants. As a result, flowers chosen by the middle and working classes reflected the kind of landscape enjoyed earlier only on the estates of the wealthy, although on a smaller scale.

The nineteenth century introduced a lively period of plant collecting both in Europe and in America. Plant explorers, mostly from Europe, often under contract with a horticultural group, a wealthy benefactor, or a nursery, traveled to Asia, Africa, and South and North America in search of new plants. Though the search was often filled with danger, uncertainty, and loneliness, plant hunting could provide a rewarding experience for the right person.

Plant hunters enabled plant collectors on America's east coast, including those in the Boston area, where greenhouses protected such treasures as the coveted orchids and camellias from the winter cold. The new flowers of the plant hunters included verbenas and petunias, a host of other half-hardy tropical roadside weeds from Brazil and Chile, geraniums from the mountainsides of South Africa, and echeverias and strange succulents from Africa's deserts.[7]

Not far from Brookline in the town of Wellesley, Horatio Hollis Hunnewell (1810–1902) displayed his collection of evergreens in a fourteen-acre pinetum, or garden of pines (fig. 3.3). In an 1867 diary entry, he stated his goal in making the garden: "It will be my aim to plant in it every conifer, native and foreign, that will be found sufficiently hardy to thrive in our cold New England climate."[8] Today, 360 towering conifers still grow in the pinetum, which is on occasion open to various groups.

Figure 3.3. Pinetum of Horatio Hollis Hunnewell (1810–1902) in Wellesley, Massachusetts, 1906. (Courtesy of the Boston Athenaeum.)

In Waltham, nine miles outside Boston, Theodore Lyman built his own greenhouses for the treasures found by the plant hunters. The Lyman Estate greenhouses are among the oldest surviving greenhouses in the United States, consisting of an 1804 grape house, an 1820 camellia house, and an 1840 orchid house.

Such wealthy Boston gardeners used their fortunes to further their interest in horticulture and enjoyed the latest plant fashion for the amateur enthusiast. Gardening on several acres demanded not only financial resources but also a staff of gardeners to carry out the work.

🐝

After 1850, however, with the rise of the suburbs, middle-class gardeners emerged, eager to learn about gardening and keep up with its trends. These homeowners, who now had a lawn to mow and a garden to cultivate, had to keep current on the latest in horticulture with more limited resources. They depended on newspapers, magazines, but especially the seed catalog, for the newest in gardening.

Philadelphia nurseryman Thomas Meehan summarized the changes in gardening when he wrote in his magazine *The Gardeners' Monthly and Horticulturist* in 1876, "Those who have now their town house for winter, and country seat for summer, are among the rarest of American citizens. Gardening at country seats is almost of the past. There is little demand for that high class of horticultural talent that this system called for. On the other hand it is a pleasure to note that suburban gardening is largely on the increase. The small places, from one to ten acres, are more numerous, we think, than they used to be."[9]

By the 1880s, suburban gardening was a growing trend. Greater affluence and leisure time allowed more homeowners a chance to travel and bring home garden ideas from England, France, and Italy. There were still drying yards, orchards, vegetable and herb gardens, but they were hidden in the rear of the property. Up front for public view were the fashionable bedding designs, garden furnishings, arbors, and summerhouses for outdoor pleasures.[10]

After the Civil War, suburbs developed where middle-class homeowners found land for a house and where they could also put down a lawn and tend a garden. Rural farmers also began to move toward the cities, where they hoped to find jobs. Historian Michael Rawson writes about the growth of the suburbs in nineteenth-century Boston, saying, "The independent pastoral suburb was more than just a new kind of place. It represented a new set of relationships between people and nature."[11] People left the cities to find that link with nature, which often meant a lawn and a garden that aligned with what seed company and nursery owners promoted. Flower beds of annuals dotted the lawn in carpet bed and ribbon designs, as demanded in the trendy Victorian style.

The Victorian decades of the nineteenth century make up three distinct periods of gardening. First came the Early Victorian, from the 1820s to 1850s, which corresponds to the formative period of Romantic garden design. The High Victorian phase, from the 1850s to the 1880s, was a time of dramatic changes in architecture and gardening, which included showy plants and flower beds. The final period, the Late Victorian, from the 1880s to about 1900, showed a mixed and a more eclectic style of home and garden.[12]

For the Victorian garden, the major change was from the Romantic landscape in the early period to a more contrived and more composite style by the end of the century.[13] Before 1850, a plain lawn with trees and shrubs was preferable to Andrew Jackson Downing rather than artifice in landscaping the home grounds: "if the proprietors of our country villas, in their improvements, are more likely to run into any one error than another, we fear it will be that of too great a desire for display—too many vases, temples, and seats,—and too little purity and simplicity of general effect."[14] He recommended a moderate use of flowers in the landscape.

That changed after 1850. The inclusion of carpet bedding and borders with colorful flowers like geraniums became the fashion. Large flowering plants like cannas and dahlias became important in the Victorian garden. In 1854, seedsman Azell Bowditch of Boston wrote in his catalog, "We shall endeavor to keep pace with the 'Flowery Age' in which we live, and hope to be able, by attention and care, to supply our patrons with all the valuable varieties of seeds that can be obtained at any other seed establishment in the Union."[15]

Nineteenth-century seed and nursery catalogs offered lawnmowers, urns, fencing, and even chickens in addition to flower seeds. They also featured instructions on how to grow flowers and in what style to display them, whether that might be in containers, flower borders, or beds. The catalogs often included an image of a suburban home with a lawn and garden, confirming what was happening around large cities across the country: people were moving to suburbs to have a lawn and a garden of flowers because they wanted to be closer to nature.

The 1881 issue of Meehan's *Gardeners' Monthly and Horticulturist* said, "As you leave the heart of the city and get out among the suburbs, you find a refined taste displayed in all the gardens surrounding the houses, both large and small, and much attention is paid to planting handsome trees and shrubs, though there is a sameness about it which the nurserymen find it hard to break up. The lawns are kept neatly shorn and carpet bedding and other more desirable styles of gardening are quite universal; showing a steady increase in the taste for such things."[16]

The number of seed companies and nurseries increased after 1870 as suburbs spread around the perimeters of large cities, and the number of men employed as seedsmen, nurserymen, and professional gardeners increased 275 percent between 1870 and 1930.[17] Suburban homes came to feature on a small scale the kind of landscapes that had surrounded the estates of the wealthy for many decades, including beds of flowers (fig. 3.4). The garden of the cottager and working class, though more limited in scale and plantings, also became a place for popular plants like the annuals, perennials, and shrubs that the middle class cultivated. At times the companies presented some products unfamiliar to the homeowner but characterized them as essential in the ads.

The catalog of the Lovett Seed Company of New Jersey claimed to offer everything the suburban gardener would need. Lovett's said that its 1882 catalog was "indispensable to all owners of country and suburban homes, whether it be a mere village lot, or the extensive grounds of the rich man's country seat."

After receiving *Vick's Illustrated Floral Guide* in 1873, Thomas Meehan wrote in his *Gardeners' Monthly and Horticulturist*: "It is a pleasure to handle so beautiful a catalogue as Mr. Vick always issues,—and then independently of its value as a seed catalogue, it is filled with directions and hints for ornamenting grounds, that it is equal to a good garden book at the same time."[18] Seed company owners like Vick became an important source of garden fashion and style—the new tastemakers (fig. 3.4).

In their 1894 company catalog, *Attractive Home Grounds*, proprietors C. P. Lines and E. F. Coe of Elm City Nursery in New Haven, Connecticut,

❧ *Figure 3.4.* A new home with flower beds on the lawn. (*Vick's Floral Guide,* 1882.)

wrote, "From the most restricted city lot to the more liberal setting of the suburban home and country estate, the possibilities of completing the effect by the judicious manipulation of nature's furnishings—her grass, shrubs, trees, with their varying tints and shades of every imaginable color and form—give possibilities that should not be neglected by any one."[19]

Though the seed companies and nurseries were there to help, the homeowner also needed an eye for art and design in the landscape. In 1881, Vick wrote in his *Vick's Illustrated Monthly* that "the residents of villages, or the suburbs of them, are most favorably situated to indulge their taste in beautifying places of moderate extent. No great wealth is necessary for this purpose, but a genuine love of art and nature."[20]

❧❧

With the rise of the horticultural industry in the late nineteenth century, the *Florist's Exchange* emerged as a weekly trade journal of "interchange for florists, nurserymen, seedsmen and the trade in general." In 1895 it noted that "a careful investigation in various lines and a direct report from the nurserymen themselves, show that, as any one section of our country becomes more thoroughly developed, cultured and refined, that section becomes an increasing buyer for the productions of the nursery."[21]

As towns, suburbs, and subdivisions expanded into the countryside, so too the nursery industries expanded to sell trees, shrubs, perennials, and annuals to a growing base of customers. At the same time, the seed companies sold even more varieties of flower seeds. Annuals were preeminently the flowers of the people. They were, after all, easily raised, quick to bloom, and inexpensive.[22]

As residents in the suburbs continued to learn about gardening from the seed and plant merchants, those merchants were eager to find new ways to connect with their customers. That connection, too, would change in ways that made more people aware of gardening methods, choices, and fashion.

In the late 1800s, significant changes in the technology of printing made promotional materials available to any business with even modest revenue. Along with an increase in the number of newspapers in cities and towns across the country, more and more magazines circulated from coast to coast. Companies that sold everything from thread to sewing machines could reach growing numbers of readers through advertisements in such publications and more effectively produce their own promotional materials to send customers across the country. At the same time, advertisements for mass-produced goods appeared on billboards, in trains and trolleys, on buildings, and even on signs scattered along country roads.

In 1873, E. Remington and Sons in New York came out with the first commercially successful typewriter. It enabled a typist to produce a block of text in standard uniform format in what was then an unbelievably short time. A new printing process, called Linotype, was invented a little over a decade later. It enabled millions of copies of newspapers, books, magazines, and catalogs to come off the press and circulate around the country. Flyers and booklets could easily be printed to publicize mass-produced products like canned food from Heinz in Pittsburgh and clothing from Marshall Field's in Chicago. The time and effort required to produce a simple letter or a newspaper would never be the same.

Mid-nineteenth-century Philadelphia seedsman Robert Buist took pride in telling his customers how his firm used the latest mass communication technologies, particularly the new Gordon letterpress. In his catalog of 1872, Buist boasted that "three of the celebrated 'Gordon's Printing Presses' are kept constantly at work on seed bags, labels, and other printing matter required in our business, and the stock of type and other printing material we use is equal in extent to that required by some of our daily papers."[23] Buist, like any businessman of that time, had to keep modern, and that meant using the latest technology to produce printed materials for his customers. He wrote in that same catalog, "When we established ourselves in 1828, the seed business in this country was in its infancy, the trade was really insignificant in comparison to what it is in the present day." The ability to print faster and distribute more widely encouraged the development of an array of new printed materials to promote the company's products, along with more advertising in national magazines.

In 1893, *Munsey's Magazine* became the first publication to base its financial success on advertising. That year, Frank Munsey changed the price of his weekly magazine from twenty-five cents per issue to ten cents. Shortly after, the number of his readers increased significantly, enabling Munsey to grow his list of advertising clients. His magazine became the first to survive on its advertising revenue rather than on subscriptions and street corner sales.

By the early 1890s, the *Ladies Home Journal* became the most successful national magazine in the country, with profits based on advertising. The extensive back pages of the magazine advertised household goods, including flower seeds from James Vick.

Cheap mail delivery proved beneficial to businesses as well. Special rates for mailing the catalogs helped make them an important sales vehicle. Large companies like Sears and Montgomery Ward, as well as seed companies and nurseries, sent out their catalogs in the millions. The garden industry had developed and now depended on a national audience for its garden products.

The emerging media, especially national magazines, made it possible to reach a wider market. Even in the late 1870s and early 1880s, while James Vick ran his company from Rochester, a national audience for his catalogs and his products was emerging. He received letters from customers around the country. A gardener from Virginia wrote, "Some who had not planted a flower since the war are taking courage and beginning again to take an interest in floriculture."[24]

❧

During the latter part of the nineteenth century, a media-generated garden appeared for the first time. People gardened according to what magazines, newspapers, and catalogs told them was important. They bought garden products described and illustrated by the same media forms.

Vick published his catalogs in German as well as English in order to reach German-speaking farmers and gardeners, an early example of how he adapted his seed catalog to influence new readers. Instructions in his 1874 catalog on how to plant vegetables provided an illustration of crops planted in straight rows (fig. 3.5). Even though it was different from how they had learned to grow vegetables in their home country, German immigrants in Wisconsin began to follow that style in their own gardens. They wanted to be recognized as gardening in the American fashion, as they saw illustrated in the Vick seed catalog.

Garden historian Marcia Carmichael, historic gardens coordinator for the living museum Old World Wisconsin, writes, "By 1880, the family kitchen garden [of German settlers in Wisconsin] showed evidence of the influences of mainstream America. Once center stage and a showpiece to the onlooker, the kitchen garden found itself relegated to the side yard. . . .

꽃 *Figure 3.5.* A vegetable garden. (*Vick's Floral Guide,* 1874.)

Plantings in neat rows replaced the traditional rectangular beds, allowing for mechanical cultivation, if desired."[25]

꽃

Vick wrote in his magazine, "Earnestly have we desired to see the people of this country appreciate the beauties of nature, study nature's laws, and, above all, love flowers and delight in their culture. . . . For a third of a century, through the press, we have kept the subject before the people, published millions of pamphlets that have reached every hamlet and almost every home in the land."[26]

But Vick often, like other business owners, had to provide newspaper editors with a press release—a notice containing information he wanted the paper to print. In the late nineteenth century, publishing press releases or notices was not a free service on the part of the newspaper. Sometimes Vick provided editors with seeds or bulbs in exchange for including a notice in the paper. An editor from a newspaper in Dansville, New York, wrote, "If it will do your benevolent heart good to know how much pleasure that box of bulbs has conferred,—and your professional mind, to know of the enlightenment to the community—why, take it as a drop in the bucket of similar praises."[27]

In his catalog as well as his magazine, Vick included testimonials from his customers. From the state of Washington, a gardener wrote, "from all sections of the country on the culture of flowers, I thought a few words from the north-western part of the United States might not be amiss . . . I have succeeded splendidly with Asters, Petunia, Portulaca, Phlox, Verbena, Larkspurs, Pansies, Antirrhinum, and, in fact, all the hardy annuals."[28]

When he received letters from customers that he thought would be of interest to other readers, he responded in his catalog or monthly magazine. Through that exchange, Vick demonstrated his skill in speaking to the needs and wants of his readers.

At his home and at his trial farm outside Rochester, Vick planted sample rows of flowers so that his customers could see the plant varieties he offered in his catalog. A reporter from the *Albany Agricultural* newspaper wrote, "The flower farm of James Vick, in the eastern suburbs of the city, has many acres devoted exclusively to flowers, including a vast collection of bulbs. . . . We found that the flowers in these beds of Pansies—which were of every imaginable shade and variegation—were literally numbered by millions."[29] In spring, Vick's display garden of tulips at his house dazzled his customers (fig. 3.6). *Horticulturist* magazine wrote, "During the blooming season the display of these and other flowers presented a brilliant and magnificent appearance."[30]

📍 *Figure 3.6.* Vick's home with fields of tulips on the south side of East Avenue. (McIntosh, *History of Monroe County*.)

Garden styles follow distinct trends. This was especially true for flowers, probably the most hallowed element of the Victorian garden, which became the subject of one of the most radical swings in garden fashion ever witnessed.[31] For most of the late nineteenth century, the model for planting flowers was seen in the habit of putting out annuals in carpet beds on the lawn (fig. 3.7). The preferred annual bedding flowers included the petunia, geranium, and lobelia. Seed catalogs like Vick's began actively promoting the use of such brightly colored annuals. A letter to Vick from South Carolina said, "The annuals germinated from the seed very readily and we had some very pretty flowers throughout the summer. Mirabilis, Zinnias and Pansies are blooming yet."[32] By the end of the century, however, an interest in perennials replaced the fashion for such annuals. Perennial or herbaceous borders then became the popular form of gardening with flowers.

FIG. 3.

✸ *Figure 3.7.* Carpet bed. (*Vick's Illustrated Monthly*, 1878.)

It was the catalog, along with the monthly magazine, that made the middle-class gardener both aware of the newest flowers and eager to buy them from a dependable seed merchant like James Vick.[33] Vick taught his customers the newest trends in gardening, including what annuals to plant. His words built both his company and the Victorian garden. Through his writing, Vick gave form to the garden as much as did the gardener on the ground who planted the seed Vick sold.

4

Women and Flowers

n the second half of the nineteenth century, as more and more home-owners were growing flowers, seed merchants turned to women as a major market. Through their catalogs, the company owners established a relationship with their female customers.

The scene Vick envisioned in his catalog and magazine focused on a woman in her garden, growing her flowers and thus enjoying a kind of closeness to the first garden of Adam and Eve. The flower garden he wrote about was a paradise that any woman could enjoy with something as simple as a packet of seeds.

It wasn't only seed merchants who painted this appealing picture of the woman gardener, nor was it a strictly American phenomenon. Both English and American garden writers of the nineteenth century encouraged women to take up gardening.

As mentioned previously, at the end of the eighteenth century and the beginning of the nineteenth, the influential English landscape gardener Humphry Repton was designing landscapes that prominently featured flower gardens. Until this time, the flower garden had played only a small role in the landscape, where it was often largely hidden. Repton wanted flowers to become an important feature. His painting of what he called a *rosarium,* or *The Rosary at Ashridge,* an intricately designed garden filled with only one flower, the rose, gives some idea of how important he felt flowers should be (fig. 4.1).[1]

England's John Claudius Loudon continued the use of flowers in his landscape designs. By the mid-nineteenth century, no serious woman gardener in England or America would have been without the book by Jane Loudon (wife of J. C. Loudon), *The Ladies' Companion to the Flower*

Figure 4.1. Humphry Repton's painting of the rosarium, *The Rosary at Ashridge* (1816). (Humphry Repton, *Fragments on the Theory and Practice of Landscape Gardening* [London: T. Bensley and Son, 1816].)

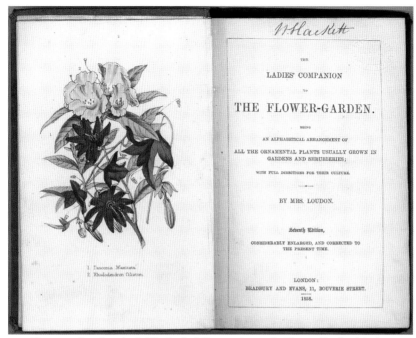

THE

LADIES' COMPANION

TO

THE FLOWER-GARDEN.

BEING

AN ALPHABETICAL ARRANGEMENT OF

ALL THE ORNAMENTAL PLANTS USUALLY GROWN IN
GARDENS AND SHRUBBERIES;

WITH FULL DIRECTIONS FOR THEIR CULTURE.

BY MRS. LOUDON.

Seventh Edition,

CONSIDERABLY ENLARGED, AND CORRECTED TO
THE PRESENT TIME.

LONDON:
BRADBURY AND EVANS, 11, BOUVERIE STREET.
1858.

1. Tacsonia Manicata
2. Rhododendron Citrinum

Figure 4.2. Jane Loudon's *The Ladies' Companion to the Flower Garden* (1841). (Courtesy of the State Library of South Australia.)

Garden (1841) (fig. 4.2), which lists many of the flowers that later numbered among the most popular in Vick's flower seed business.

Jane Loudon was already a published author when she met her future husband, but it was he who taught her about gardening. She worked with him on his own books, magazine, and articles. It is largely to Jane that we owe the Victorian era's deeply ingrained belief that for every English woman, having a garden is all about growing flowers.

In the 1870s, English gardener Sophia Orne Johnson wrote in her book, *Every Woman Her Own Flower Gardener,* that "a small set of tools, comprising a rake and hoe on one handle, a trowel, and a spade, are very essential. With their aid much light work can be accomplished without calling upon Mr. O'Shovelem. . . . With these implements, every woman can be her own gardener—and not only raise all the flowers she may desire, but also contribute a large share of the vegetables that are always welcomed at the table, during both summer and winter."[2]

American garden historian Beverly Seaton has pointed out that men certainly helped with the heavy digging and other tasks in the Victorian-era garden, but the woman was the gardener: "The role of the male in the woman's flower garden was that of the animated shovel, or as Sophia Johnson called him in the nineteenth century, 'Mr. O'Shovelem.'"[3]

Women also became major garden writers for other women. They Americanized the garden advice of Gertrude Jekyll and William Robinson, the most popular and influential English garden writers at the end of the nineteenth century.[4]

English garden historian Jeffrey Taylor wrote of the nineteenth century, "It is true that the day of the professional woman gardener was still in the future, but though two or three of the outstanding men gardeners of the century were professionals, the great majority were amateurs; and, among the practical amateurs, the women were as eminent as the men."[5]

❧

At the beginning of the nineteenth century, English gardeners could not get enough of the new plants coming into the country. The question for many became, "Where do I plant them?" After years of stately lawns surrounding the manor house, there seemed little space to showcase these latest garden novelties. Lady Anne Grenville would offer a solution that changed flower gardens forever.

Lady Anne's husband, Lord William Wyndham Grenville, began his political career in the House of Commons in 1782, becoming prime minister in 1806. The next year, he was successful in passing a law that abolished the slave trade. Lord and Lady Grenville's country estate, Dropmore House, boasted an extensive landscape. By 1825, Lady Anne felt frustrated that she had no room for the new plants coming from abroad. Mr. Frost, her gardener, suggested cutting large circles in a lawn that fronted the drawing-room windows and filling them with the new flowering plants. He planted several scarlet bergamots, blue salvias, and yellow cosmos, thus breaking a century's taboo—dictating that it was not proper to include more than one kind of plant in a bed—and starting a colossal new garden fashion.[6]

By the mid-nineteenth century, English gardeners had invented carpet bedding, using low-growing plants to create a design on the lawn, which might take the shape of a star, a half moon, or circle. Victorian America loved the new carpet bedding and took this form of planting to new heights, using three-dimensional wire shapes, like a ball or an animal, and covering them with plants. In 1889, reports arrived in England about these three-dimensional forms and were greeted with pious wishes that an art so debased should never reach the English shores.[7]

Garden books for women began to appear more regularly on the market. Louisa Johnson, an English gardener, in 1839 wrote a book for women called *Every Lady Her Own Flower Gardener* (not to be confused with Sophia Orne Johnson's *Every Woman Her Own Flower Gardener,* mentioned above). It was a response to another book by Jane Loudon, *The Young Lady's Book of Botany* (1838), which focused on plant science and learning the Latin names of plants. Johnson wrote about flowers, or as she called it, "floriculture," a term that Vick often used in both his catalog and his magazine.

With such support, nineteenth-century American women gardeners cultivated flowers with a sense that they were doing more than simply growing pansies. They were attempting to establish a sense of identity as well.

The love of flowers as a part of God's creation motivated many women during the Victorian nineteenth century. Flowers, linked by some to a natural theology of that time, reflected God's love. The flower was intended by God as a creature of joy and beauty for the human soul. Thus, there was more to the love of the flower than simply a natural draw to its color and form. It was the duty of all to honor God by treasuring his creatures, the flowers.

Nicolette Scourse, in her book *The Victorians and Their Flowers,* says that "it had long been an accepted fact 'that the most highly adorned productions of Flora's kingdom were called into existence' only at the appearance of man and his intellect capable of contemplating floral beauty."[8] She is quoting here James M'Cosh and George Dickie, from their *Typical Forms and Special Ends in Creation* (1856), who were in turn drawing upon the natural theology of William Paley (1743–1805), English philosopher and clergyman.

Paley's *View of the Evidences of Christianity* described creation as a reflection of divinity. Charles Darwin had been required to read Paley's book *Natural Theology* when he studied at Christ's College. Darwin, who carried out extensive research on plants as well as, more famously, on the evolution of animal species, admired Paley's clear use of words and, most of all, his use of evidence and logic.[9] Paley argued that we could learn about God through his creatures, and such a doctrine in natural theology persisted for decades in philosophizing about the natural world.

Louisa Johnson provided a bit of English garden history as a means to emphasize the importance of the garden experience for women. She wrote, "Queen Anne remodeled the gardens of Kensington, and did away with the Dutch inventions [topiary]. Hampton Court was also laid out in a more perfect state in her reign, under the direction of [landscape gardener Henry] Wise. Since that period, flower-gardening has progressed rapidly; and the amusement of floriculture has become the dominant passion of the ladies of Great Britain."[10]

Women's relationship to flowers was explained in various ways. Some claimed that flowers presented an opportunity for a woman to develop an interest in science, particularly botany. She could learn the science of the flower, and thus exercise her intellectual curiosity. The other common view of women's interest in flowers hinged on the emotional impact of the flower on the senses. According to Jane Loudon, women, as creatures ruled by emotions and senses, would delight in growing, collecting, and even drying flowers.

American writer Sarah Josepha Hale also encouraged women to study botany and cultivate an interest in flowers. The July 1841 issue of the magazine she edited, *Godey's Lady's Book,* stated that the preservation of wild flowers was "a subject worthy the attention of our sex" and characterized the benefits of this activity as "a pleasing exercise for the mind."[11]

Even more significant, Hale pointed to such activity as an example of women's civic involvement. Such botanizing efforts, she suggested, would save America's floral treasures from the relentless march of civilization. Women could help preserve America's native plants, a most worthy goal. The limitations of nineteenth-century American women's role seem in many ways also to have enabled a certain dedication to flowers.[12] Thus, the garden emerged as a stronghold of freedom and self-identity.

❦

House plants would help during the cold of winter, but they needed a certain setting with the proper water and light. For this time of year, the Victorians encouraged indoor plants. Harriet Beecher Stowe, in a book cowritten with her sister Catherine Esther Beecher, *The American Woman's Home* (1869), recommended growing house plants to help bring humidity to the dry winter air in the house. The authors included a black-and-white illustration showing a detail of window and plants (fig. 4.3).

❦

For several decades during the nineteenth century, Martha Turnbull kept a diary of her garden at her Louisiana plantation, Rosedown, located in Saint Francisville, West Feliciana Parish. She began the diary in 1836, the year she put in the garden, writing in detail about what she planted on her twenty-eight acres (though the plantation itself was much larger).

Her diary illustrates how horticulture, especially home gardening, changed over the decades of the nineteenth century. In the earlier years, she focused on practical herbs and vegetables and fruit, especially strawberries. Later, her concern turned to ornamental gardening, incorporating beds and

Figure 4.3. Nineteenth-century indoor gardening. (Beecher and Stowe, *The American Woman's Home.*)

borders of perennials and annuals, with roses, dahlias, and chrysanthe-mums playing a central role.[13] Through the decades, that garden would produce an abundance of flowers.

৬২

From the earliest years of the nineteenth century, women's interest in and association with flowers and floriculture had flourished, largely due to the influence of women writers, who supported it with religious, civic, and emotional appeals.

Vick would use his seed catalog and magazine to feed that fascination, specifically encouraging women to pursue horticulture. A woman gardener from Missouri wrote him in 1878, "Nothing gives me greater pleasure than the culture of flowers. . . . I feel proud of our flowers. I give you the praise."[14] Another from California wrote to Vick and said, "No other florist has done so much to create a love for flowers, and we ladies all give you a vote of thanks."[15]

Toward the end of his life, reminiscing on his work in the seed business for the past twenty-five years, Vick wrote of his success in spreading that love of flowers, especially among women. "To any one who can look back a quarter of a century, the increase of a love for flowers and their cultivation within that time seems almost marvelous."[16]

5

❧ ❧

Flower Garden Fashion

wners of seed companies and nurseries often went as far as to write books to share their knowledge. A prominent example was Joseph Breck (1794–1873), who began his business in Boston in 1818. For several years, Breck worked on a book about flower gardening, which he called *The Flower Garden, or Breck's Book of Flowers, in Which Are Described All the Various Hardy Herbaceous Perennials, Annuals, Shrubby Plants, and Evergreen Trees, Desirable for Ornamental Purposes, with Directions for Their Cultivation.* After first publication in 1851, it went through several editions. Breck had incorporated much of the material from his earlier articles in *Horticultural Register, New England Farmer,* and the *Horticulturist.* He also drew on the works of other English and American horticulturists, including John Claudius Loudon's *Encyclopedia of Plants.*

Breck began with the placement of the flower garden, which he felt should be located before a window with southern or southeastern exposure. "The principle on which it is laid out ought to be that of exhibiting a variety of colors and forms so blended as to produce one beautiful whole. In a small flower-garden, viewed from the windows of the house, this effect is best produced by beds, or borders, formed on the side of each other, and parallel to the windows from whence they are seen."[1]

He carefully laid out for the reader examples of flower bed design. The layout could be in a rectangular shape with smaller plots inside, a walkway, and a border around the entire garden. He advised that "this outward border will be the most appropriate place for choice flowering shrubs, and tall herbaceous biennial and perennial plants."[2] He particularly suggested boxwood shrubs as an edging for the garden. Of course, they needed to be kept trimmed, to complement the flowers.

The gravel walk should be four feet wide, to allow two people to walk side by side. Its first layer should be stony rubbish, broken bricks, or small stones. On top of that, he suggested the placement of six to eight inches of gravel. Breck also recommended a roller to keep the gravel path in place: "A garden roller is indispensable where there is any extent of walks, and it should be applied as often as once a week, and particularly after a rain."[3]

As for what flowers to plant, Breck listed several annuals, plus a few choice perennials, including the rose. He also promoted native plants, because they were often overlooked in favor of imported varieties. "Many beautiful plants may be selected from the woods and fields, by those who wish to ornament their grounds at the least expense. These would be more highly prized than many far-fetched plants, that are trumpeted before the public." He proposed such natives as *Lobelia cardinalis, Aquilegia canadensis, Aster novae-angliae,* and *Solidago,* concluding that "surely, in making up our selections of plants, those of our own native land should not be neglected."[4]

Breck's goal was to have a garden in which something was blooming during each season. Choosing the right plants would provide ongoing color for the garden. Therefore, his beds and borders were filled with an array of appropriate annuals, perennials, and native plants.

Later, New York seedsman Peter Henderson (1822–90) wrote the first edition of his book *Gardening for Pleasure: A Guide to the Amateur in the*

Fruit, Vegetable, and Flower Garden (1875). In it he also discussed laying out the flower garden and the choice of plants.

He noted at the start that old-fashioned mixed borders with hardy herbaceous plants were "now but little seen." He wrote, "The mixed system still has its advocates, who deprecate the modern plan of massing in color as being too formal, and too unnatural a way to dispose of flowers."[5] The fashion of the moment, carpet bedding, called for the dense planting of many flowers of the same variety to create a display of one color to fit whatever the design the gardener had cut into the lawn. Thus, the plants Henderson recommended were generally annuals, because they would provide color throughout the season through continual bloom.

For example, a circular bed with a ten-foot diameter would have required eight or ten different kinds of plants to form the contrast of smaller, concentric circles of different colors within the larger circle. The plants, of course, needed to be kept trimmed to just a few inches to keep the look of massed color. Henderson recommended that the center plants stand at the highest point, and the plants around the circle's edge at the lowest point. These might include a *Canna* in the center and shorter plants like *Coleus* and *Alternanthera* in the outer circles. This "modern flower garden," as it was called at the time, could require hundreds of plants of a single variety to create the necessary color mass. As Henderson wrote, "A single misplaced color may spoil the effect of the whole."[6]

Thus, within a span of only twenty-five years, Breck and Henderson prescribed two entirely different forms of the flower bed for their readers. Breck advocated a bed of mixed annuals and perennials and encouraged the incorporation of native plants, whereas Henderson advised the modern carpet bed based on mass planting with mainly annuals, including exotics from other countries. James Vick also became one of carpet bedding's most devoted supporters.

In 1888, the *American Agriculturalist* included an article called "Our Flower Garden the Coming Season," which noted the distinction between the old garden of perennial borders and the modern garden style with

Figure 5.1. Flower bed on the lawn. (*American Agriculturist*, 1888.)

annuals. "Until about fifty years ago . . . the 'mixed border' was the general style in which gardens were laid out and planted. About that time the bedding system was introduced. . . . In this, plants of low stature are planted close together, so that their flowers produce masses of contrasting or harmonizing colors" (fig. 5.1).[7]

A year later, Rochester nurseryman George H. Ellwanger wrote in favor of a return to hardy flower borders and masses of stately perennials. Like other gardeners of that time, he was probably feeling the need for an old-fashioned kind of garden which demanded less maintenance than a bed of annuals. The mixed mode of bedding survived in rather specialized areas of gardening until the end of the nineteenth century.[8]

❧

Flowers were important in the landscape, but were planted according to the style of the period. By the end of the century—the High Victorian period— flowers were colorful and spread around the property in vases, beds, borders, and ever more intricate designs on the lawn. By then even three-dimensional designs that used plants with colorful leaves or flowers were popular.

It was the love of those flowers that Vick sought to cultivate. In 1879 he included in his magazine a letter titled "All Need the Flowers" from a customer in Ottawa, Illinois, who wrote, "Who needs flowers most, the old or the young? has long been a mooted question in my mind. Flowers are the symbols of all that are pure and true in this life, and they teach us to hope for Life to come."[9]

❧ *Figure 5.2.* Geranium. (*Vick's Magazine*, 1882.)

6

The Vick Seed Company

Founded on Flowers

ick built his company on the central role of flowers in the garden, envisioning a scene in which flowers would contribute to the well-being of gardeners everywhere. He wrote that "in all parts of the civilized world, the refinement, and innocence, and happiness of the people may be measured by the flowers they cultivate."[1]

Shortly after Vick arrived in Rochester in 1837, the city had become home to several seed companies and nurseries, and by midcentury it had earned the nickname "Flower City." Agriculture and horticulture had become powerful forces in the economy of the city. Nurserymen owned or leased nearly two thousand acres within a ten-mile radius of the Four Corners, the center of downtown.[2] Greenhouses, together with ornamental trees and shrubs, covered the nurseries' fields. Flowers grew in abundance, too, in the trial fields of a booming seed trade that would also contribute to Rochester's new image.

The name "Flower City" reflected the good soil and climate, but just as important were its transportation links to other cities, both east and west. The Erie Canal, stretching across northern New York State, opened in 1825 and made Rochester a shipping port for commercial goods. Later, arrival of the railroad enabled the rapid movement of products, including plants and seeds, across the country. The largest and most famous nursery in the city, Ellwanger and Barry, which opened in 1840, owed its success to the easy access to a national market. After the 1860s, the nursery opened a branch in California to sell its trees and shrubs to new homeowners in the far west. Other local seed companies filled orders and shipped them by mail to gardeners wherever they lived. Later in his career, Vick even owned his own rail car for shipping his seeds.

The city of Rochester also became home to other businesses that supported the garden industry, like printing and lithography, examples of the latter being the Rochester Lithograph Company and firm owned by bookseller and illustrator Dellon Marcus Dewey. In chromolithography, as it was formally called, an artist would first paint a scene. Another artist would reproduce that image, etching it into stone. The stone then would be coated with various colors of ink, and the artist would press a piece of paper over the etchings to produce a paper copy of the original painting.

By the end of the century, the city of Rochester had become famous for its chromos of botanical art. In the early 1890s, local printers and artists published a magazine called *Botanical Art* to show the world the splendid chromolithographs of the trees, shrubs, and flowers that came from Rochester's nurseries and seed houses.

In late nineteenth-century America, it was not uncommon for companies to sell chromolithographs, which became a popular way for middle-class families to display art in their homes. Vick was an early adopter of chromolithography for his business, offering a series of flower chromos (fig. 6.1) in his catalog and magazine. By framing the chromo and hanging it up in the parlor or dining room, customers could enjoy Vick's flowers throughout the year. Vick used this art form to depict flowers as a possibility for every home. He saw the color and shape of flowers as providing

comfort and beauty to everyone willing to invest the time and effort in growing them.

Each of Vick's chromos depicted a vase, basket, or bouquet filled with flowers. In his 1874 catalog Vick wrote, "We have already sold over one hundred thousand of these Chromos without a penny of profit, nor do we desire one. They have performed their mission—increased the love of flowers, made more pleasant the homes of our customers, and we are more than satisfied."[3] Vick's chromos cost a customer one dollar, which covered the printing and postage. The chromo was printed "on strong paper, sized and varnished, and sent by mail, postage paid." He emphasized the chromos' value when he wrote, "In this style the Chromo is equal to an oil painting." If a customer wanted the chromo framed, that was also available: "We offer Chromos Framed in Black Walnut and Gilt at $3.00 each."[4] Through the many years of his business, Vick continued the practice. In his catalog of 1880, for example, he advertised the chromos inside the front cover, writing, "For the purpose of increasing the love of Flowers, we have prepared several very beautiful Floral Chromos—all drawn from nature, and every flower of natural size and color."[5]

Chromos were also an effective means of selling products. Vick's 1864 catalog, for example, featured a lithograph of new double zinnias, which had been developed just four years earlier.[6] The use of color helped Vick illustrate the detail in the flowers to his many customers across the country. Philadelphia nurseryman Thomas Meehan wrote in his magazine *Gardeners' Monthly and Horticulturist* in 1880, "We believe the money spent in printer's ink for the two pages a colored plate occupies, would not be half as telling as the colored illustrations of the thing itself. We have no doubt this style of advertising will grow."[7] And grow it did, until photography took center stage in product promotion.

Through this new form of advertising, the garden industry gave the world illustrations that have become colorful heirloom treasures that

❧ *Figure 6.1.* Chromo D. Vase containing thirty-six winter flowering bulbs. (*Vick's Floral Guide,* 1874.)

people still appreciate and collect. Today, when people think about nine-teenth-century seed and nursery catalogs, the colored chromolithograph illustrations on the cover and within the catalog, as well as on the seed packet, often come to mind.

❧

In 1856, Vick began his seed business, first selling imported French flower seeds to his friends. He later conducted the business from his home located on East Avenue on the site of the Old Union Tavern and Race Course, which he acquired in 1866. Today the two streets that once formed the long sections of the oval racecourse are called Vick Park A and Vick Park B.

The East Avenue house, at what today is the location of Saint Paul's Epis-copal Church (fig. 6.2), served as the Vick homestead from 1866 to 1888. He lived there with his wife, the former Mary Elizabeth Seelye, and their children. The Vicks had three daughters and five sons, one of whom died in early child-hood. Vick planted peonies and other flowers on the south side of his house, along East Avenue. His gardens, which covered much of the twenty-three acres, were among Rochester's showplaces and tourist attractions.[8]

❧ *Figure 6.2.* Vick's house on East Avenue. (Courtesy of the Rochester Historical Society.)

In the spring of 1867, more than a hundred thousand tulips bloomed in Vick's home garden. Throughout the summer and fall, the garden featured annuals like zinnias, phlox, asters, verbenas, cockscombs, petunias, portulaca, balsams, pansies, and many other varieties.[9] All were essential features in the Victorian garden of that time. As a hybridizer, Vick made notable advances in the crossbreeding of flowers. Among his creations were the white double phlox, fringed petunia, white gladiolus, and Japanese cockscomb.[10]

Vick's home gardens attracted so many visitors that he decided in 1870 to move his seed packaging and distribution to a four-story warehouse and store on State and Market Streets in downtown Rochester (figs. 6.3 and 6.4).

Figure 6.3. Vick seed house, downtown Rochester, 1873. (*Vick's Illustrated Floral Guide,* 1873.)

At the same time, he also planted flowers on a seventy-five-acre tract he had bought about five miles north of Rochester, in Irondequoit on Lake Ontario. That became his new trial garden, which his brothers Joseph and William supervised.

By 1875, he had built large greenhouses at his seed farm, where he could grow both flowers and vegetables. Over the years, his trial gardens also continued to attract visitors. One customer wrote, "In addition to a correspondence of sixteen years, it has twice been my happy lot to visit your beautiful flower-fields; (garden is too small a word for this occasion)."[11]

Vick wanted his customers to enjoy a healthy indoor home life, with flowering plants inside as well as a garden of flowers outside. A Wisconsin customer wrote, "Mr. Vick: Do you really wish to create a 'love of flowers among the million'? . . . The 'millions' are living now in darkened, ill-ventilated,

☙ *Figure 6.4.* Storefront of the Vick Seed Company, 1873. (*Vick's Illustrated Floral Guide*, 1873.)

ill-drained houses, eating bad food, and breathing bad air sweetly and patiently as if there could never be anything better. You, Mr. Vick, have these masses by the nose, florally speaking, and if you choose you can lead them out into a wider, higher and more cheerful existence."[12] Such words must have challenged Vick to pursue his goals even more firmly. He was helping people in their everyday experience, giving them a chance to lead a better, healthier life.

Vick's seed business reflected the Victorian focus on decoration both inside and outside the home. Throughout his career, Vick offered seeds for outdoor growing but also included in his catalog plants that a homeowner might use to decorate the interior. Eventually he would sell flowerpots along with shelving to showcase interior plants like ferns, which had come into fashion.

❧

After 1875, wealthier middle-class homes often featured turrets and a wraparound porch that sometimes circled the whole house. Designs in wood appeared above the porch railing, which also had its share of decorative work. The porches, of course, were covered in vines, including the popular morning glory, whose flowers brought colors of white, red, purple, and blue to the walls of the house or garden structure (fig. 6.5).

To help with such decoration in the Victorian landscape, Vick offered many varieties of flowers, both annual and perennial. The fashions associated with flowers sometimes assumed the most extravagant and bizarre proportions.[13] Vick produced a hybrid *Amaranthus* called 'Sunrise.' This tall annual, with its brightly colored clusters of flowers, became a popular choice for Victorian flower beds (fig. 6.6).

In providing plants for the interior of the house, he recommended a window garden, a spot the homeowner could close off with glass doors to protect the plants. He wanted indoor gardening to give as much pleasure to the homeowner as the flower garden would do in the summer. For those who could afford them, Vick also spoke of the value of a conservatory or

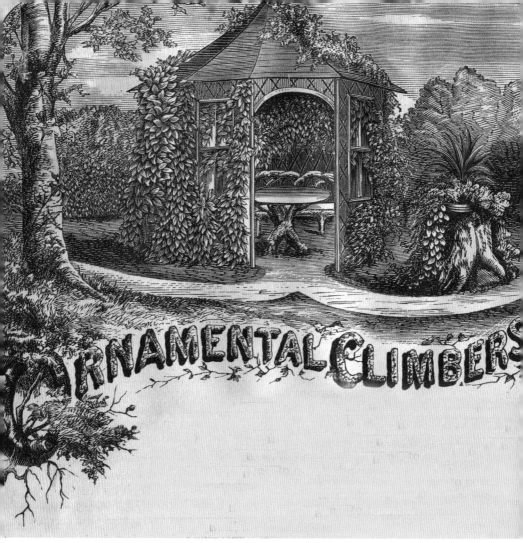

Figure 6.5. Ornamental climbers. (*Vick's Floral Guide,* 1873.)

Figure 6.6. *Amaranthus* 'Sunrise.' (*Vick's Monthly Magazine,* 1878.)

 Figure 6.7. Conservatory. (*Parker and Wood* seed catalog. Courtesy of the Warshaw Collection of Business Americana: Seed Industry and Trade, Archives Center, National Museum of American History, Smithsonian Institution.)

greenhouse attached to the home: "Private conservatories are made for pleasure, and should be arranged somewhat in the manner of a garden, with a few large and beautiful plants, and broad walks, where the proprietor and his family can lounge away an hour pleasantly, in a measure free from care" (fig. 6.7).[14]

❧

People recognized the role that Vick played in encouraging the gardener to grow flowers. In 1870, historian George Rowell wrote, "The progress and refinement of a people are made evident by their home surroundings as much as by their dress, scientific and social accomplishments, and religious regard for the Creator. The man, therefore, who honestly disseminates the seeds of flowers and plants with which to adorn the homes of the land is one of God's own ministers of good to man. Such a man is James Vick of Rochester, New York."[15]

Vick wrote in his catalog of 1877, "Our desire is to reach the whole people, and exert an influence for good in every village and hamlet, and we would like to have a place in every house."[16] He was evidently successful in this endeavor, for the Vick Seed Company continued to dominate the flower trade in America well into the 1890s.[17]

A Michigan customer wrote in 1879, "I think you are doing a good work, cultivating the love of flowers among all classes. You have done me a great deal of good."[18] By focusing on flowers, Vick defined his link to his customers, his way of relating to them. Gardeners in the Victorian period loved flowers, and Vick not only encouraged that love but helped create and nurture that love through his own words. Vick chose a way to relate to his customers that would put their interests at the center of his business, spreading floriculture and enabling a better life for his many readers. He wrote, "I feel far more than a commercial interest in the success of those to whom I furnish seeds, sympathizing with all both in success and failure, and making every possible effort to insure success."[19]

Vick's vision of flowers spread around the country and expressed what his business had set out to do: share his love of flowers with others. He enjoyed growing flowers at his house in Rochester, and he simply wanted to share that experience with others and contribute to an environment that everyone could enjoy. As he wrote, "The love and care of flowers is one of the few pleasures that improve alike the head and the heart. It is a pleasure that brings no pain, a sweet without a snare."[20]

American garden writer Rose Standish Nichols wrote in 1902, "A love of flowers is the natural foundation on which to build all gardens whether formal or informal."[21] Her sentiment summed up what had been happening in the garden since the 1850s, when the idea that gardening was for more than vegetables first gained traction beyond the groomed estates of the wealthy. Any homeowner, including a farmer, could enjoy a garden filled with flowers such as one of Vick's favorites, the annual phlox (fig. 6.8). Vick wrote, "If the farmer neglects the culture of flowers in his own garden and door-yard, where, in the country, can his children find such Eden-spots?"[22]

෩෩ *Figure 6.8.* Annual phlox. (*Vick's Monthly Magazine,* 1880.)

7

The Garden Catalog

Means of Business

he primary way that James Vick, like other entrepreneurs in the seed and plant industry of the time, could reach customers spread across the country was through the words of his catalog. It was the one tool that made the business possible and the vehicle through which the business succeeded or failed.

Vick often wrote about the power of his catalog to bring his message to his customers. He said in 1878, "Our readers know how earnestly we have labored to encourage the culture of flowers, being especially anxious that the young, and the poor and unfortunate should learn something of the soothing, refining and enriching power of beauty."[1]

The catalog included a list of seeds and bulbs available for sale, whether of annuals, perennials, biennials, or vegetables (fig. 7.1). The Vick Seed Company offered seed packets, just like every other seed company at that time, but Vick had to impress upon his customers that his seed was of a

TABLE OF CONTENTS.

For the convenience of our customers we have arranged the different classes of flowers in DEPARTMENTS, so that with a little care in examining our GUIDE no one will be *guided* wrong, but can select just the kind of seeds or plants needed for any particular purpose. Sad mistakes are made for want of this knowledge, by those who commence the culture of flowers, and for whose success we are particularly anxious.

ANNUALS, and all seeds that produce flowers the first summer from seed sown in the spring, will be found described and arranged alphabetically, commencing with *Adonis*, page 10, and ending with *Zinnia*, page 28, ... 10–28

In the Department of PERENNIALS we describe all those flowers that bloom the second summer after the seed is sown, while the plants endure Northern winters, and continue to live on for years, like the Perennial Larkspur, (Delphinium,) Hollyhock, &c., ... 38–43

CLIMBERS, embracing the Climbing Plants that come to perfection and flower the first summer after seed is sown, ... 29–31

Under the heading GREENHOUSE will be found all those seeds that require house or greenhouse culture, like the Chinese Primrose, Chrysanthemum, etc., ... 44, 45

In this Department we give descriptions of *Everlasting Flowers*, that is, those flowers that can be picked when in bud or flower, and by merely drying for a few days in the shade will retain both form and color for many years. All thus described can be grown from seed with ordinary care. Also, descriptions of the *Ornamental Grasses*, to be treated in the same way, ... 32–34

In this Department, BULBS AND PLANTS, we make two parts, *Hardy Bulbs and Plants*, including all that will endure a Northern winter, like Lilies, Pæonies, etc., in the open ground, and *Tender Bulbs and Plants*, including those bulbs that must be kept from frost over winter, like Gladiolus, Dahlia, etc., and Geraniums, Fuchsias, and other house plants. Also, plants for Ornamental Flower Beds, like Coleus, Centaureas, etc.

HARDY BULBS AND PLANTS, ... 46–53
TENDER BULBS AND PLANTS, ... 54, 72
PLANTS FOR ORNAMENTAL BEDS—$1.00 Collections, 72

DRY FLOWERS AND GRASSES, many persons prefer to purchase rather than to grow, as they can obtain a nice collection for winter at a moderate price, while there are some very beautiful that cannot be grown in all places. For descriptions and prices of Dry Flowers, Baskets and Bouquets, see pages 35–37

The description of VEGETABLES commences at page 73, with *Artichoke*, and continues alphabetically nearly through the book, followed by the Sweet Herbs, Grasses and Clover, and a few pages devoted to descriptions of some of the most useful Garden Implements, Fancy Flower Pots, Vases, and other Ornamental Goods.

Figure 7.1. Seed, bulb, and plant offerings in *Vick's Floral Guide*, 1880.

better quality than that sold in any other catalog or local general store. His writing would spell out that difference.

Seeds from peddlers' carts and country stores were often scorned because they were often not true to the name on the packet. Merchants who sold through mail-order catalogs insisted that "'they [seeds in general stores] are not so certain to be pure and fresh'—purchase from the new mail-order catalogs."[2] The catalog provided a more efficient means for the seed companies to sell their product, and the government even provided favorable post office rates for sending seed packets across the country.

One of Vick's customers from Illinois wrote, "I would say that I am compelled to believe that there is one honest seed-dealer, at least, in the world, and I would like your photograph for my Album, so that I can see how a real-live-honest seedsman looks."[3] Though it took Vick much time to fill the frequent requests for his photo, he enjoyed the trust of his customers.

People loved the catalogs for many reasons, which they openly expressed in letters to Vick: contact with the owner, words of encouragement, learning about gardening, but above all because of the quality of the seeds. One of Vick's customers testified to that quality in these words: "I have learned more about the cultivation of flowers and Vegetables in your Catalogues than in all the other books and journals I have ever read. I have the most beautiful flower garden that I know of for miles around."[4]

The publishing industry changed between 1830 and 1870 with the introduction of new printing technology, and this technology, in turn, introduced a new model for the traditional medium of the catalog. It is instructive to take the example of two garden businesses, one run by William Kenrick in Boston and the other by James Vick in New York, which operated at the far ends of the time span and produced two different kinds of catalog. In each case, however, the catalog served the same function, linking the seller to his customers.

William Kenrick (1795–1872) inherited his nursery business from his father, who had started it in the late 1700s, selling fruit trees, ornamental trees, and shrubs to customers throughout New England. Kenrick ran the nursery successfully from the 1820s till 1850, when he sold off the land on which the nursery stood and closed the business. The property was located in a small town called Newton, five and a half miles from the center of Boston and one-half mile from the Great Western Railroad. From a central office in Boston, he would ship his customers' orders to anywhere in the country.

Kenrick's catalog (or broadsheet) was mainly a listing of plants for sale, with nothing more than the name and the price for each plant. In the 1828 catalog, Kenrick even admitted, "In this list many annual species are omitted, they being of little import, but seeds of them will be supplied if desired." Though the catalog was thin, it was the standard printed means most nurseries and seed companies used at that time.

In 1832, the catalog cover read simply, "Catalogue of Fruit and Hardy Ornamental Trees, Shrubs, Herbaceous Plants, etc." The paper was quite thin, the printing was entirely in black ink, and the entries lacked illustrations of any kind. In that year, Kenrick started the catalog with a short letter to his customers called "Introductory Observations." A year later he renamed that opening section "Advertisement," a term that other nurserymen had begun to use as well. His writing was brief, direct, and to the point.

Kenrick limited his remarks to this opening section, which he placed on the inside of the front cover. You never heard his voice in the remainder of the catalog. He did not describe the benefits of a particular plant—though he sold many varieties—or include planting instructions. It was as if the products he sold would speak for themselves.

By 1874, when seedsman James Vick published the ninth edition of his catalog, there were considerable differences in both the content and format (fig. 7.2). Around this time, he increased the editions of *Vick's Illustrated Catalogue and Floral Guide* from two to four per year, largely since he felt he had more to say to his customers about gardening with flowers.

The cover, though in black and white, was illustrated with flowers. It was the time of High Victorian style in America, and intricate floral artwork on the cover was sure to offer a certain appeal to his customers.

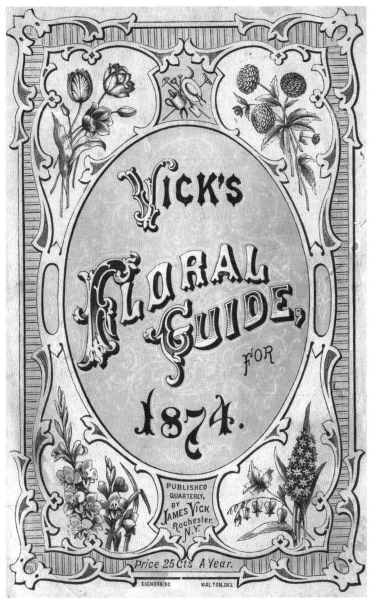

Figure 7.2. Flowery front cover of Vick's seed catalog, 1874.

Inside the front cover, Vick listed the contents of the catalog, including the titles and page numbers of the short articles. The actual listing of plants did not begin for almost thirty pages. As Vick discussed each plant, usually with an illustration, he would describe it and emphasize its value for the gardener. Other seed companies used similar formats, but none as successfully as Vick's. For example, the contents of New York's Peter Henderson and Company seed catalog in the 1870s resembled Vick's, with one exception, the number of engravings. Vick's had many more. He wrote at the time, "It is my desire to give an engraving of every flower and plant described, for I find it very difficult to convey a correct idea of the appearance of a flower or the habits of a plant by words only."[5]

It is no surprise that the seed and nursery catalogs of today seek to include as many images as possible in order to persuade readers that a particular flower *must* be among their selection for the coming season. Gardeners love illustrations. Vick wrote, "My customers and the Press have received the Floral Guide with satisfaction, as is quite evident from the many pleasant and complimentary words which I receive from various sources. By some it is characterized as the most neat and tasteful work of the kind either in Europe or America, and as remarkable for its usefulness as its beauty."[6]

The major difference between Kenrick's and Vick's approaches to catalogs was that in Vick's case, the catalog was a means of relating to customers rather than simply a listing of products. He subsequently developed the magazine to reinforce that relationship with his customers and so that he could discuss in more detail their questions and concerns. As he summed it up, "Nothing affords me so much pleasure as to know that my customers succeed and feel well repaid for the time and money spent to procure fine flowers."[7]

❧

In 1871, Vick wrote, "Of the editions [of the catalog] of 1870, more than one hundred and forty thousand were circulated, and my arrangements are made for printing two hundred thousand of this number."[8] A year later he wrote, "To my nearly two hundred thousand customers and friends, I return most heartfelt thanks for their continued confidence."[9] The number of his customers continued to increase on a regular yearly basis.

He was not at all modest in letting his customers know that they were receiving a seed catalog of the highest quality in both content and visual appeal: "I feel pleasure in sending you the *Floral Guide* for 1872, because I think you will acknowledge that it is not only valuable, giving more real instruction than can be found in any other work of the kind, but that it is really beautiful, worthy of a place in any library or parlor in the land."[10]

In 1880, he wrote in the introduction to his catalog, "For a quarter of a century my Floral Guide has made its annual visits to hundreds of thousands of people. It is found in almost every house from the Atlantic to the Pacific—on the rugged, rocky eastern coast, on the fertile prairies, and among the mountains and canyons of the Pacific coast."[11]

Vick built his credibility on his experience as both a writer and a horticulturist, saying, "Our long connection with the Horticultural Press had made us familiar with the condition of American taste and the wants and wishes of the lovers of flowers. It may also have given the people some confidence in our ability to teach them wisely."[12]

Within the first thirty pages of his catalog, before the listing of seeds, Vick often included articles like "Floral Decorations," "Rockeries," "Money Value of Flowers," "Information for the People," "Our Chromos," "Treatment of Vases and Baskets," "Ordering Seeds and Forwarding Money," and "Horticultural Books." The catalog was a way for Vick to instruct his readers as well as list his seeds for sale. In the section on books, he recommended Sophia Orne Johnson's popular *Every Woman Her Own Flower Gardener*. Vick's catalog included several black-and-white drawings of plants but also other illustrations, such as a home parlor decorated in plants, frames for flower designs, a summer cottage, and dinner table ornaments.

As already seen, he sometimes answered particular letters he had received. He once wrote, "We find the difficulties experienced by one are usually shared by thousands."[13] The letters poured in. The busy spring season might see as many as three thousand a day.[14]

The back of the inside front covers of Vick's catalogs listed the printer E. R. Andrews and electrotype setter James Lennox, both of Rochester. Andrews printed catalogs for the seed and nursery trade. Lennox incorporated electrotyping to prepare the material for printing, a process invented in the late 1830s. By the end of the century, it had become a standard method for producing plates for letterpress printing. Vick also turned to the printer Adolph Nolte, who printed some of the chromos that Vick made available to his customers.

Through the catalog at first, Vick enjoyed an ongoing relationship with his customers. It was not long before his customers wrote to Vick, requesting that he start a magazine that would be issued monthly. Vick heard that request and finally, in 1878, he responded in a way that would make his customers even more faithful to him and his business: he began publication of *Vick's Illustrated Monthly.* He wrote, "We furnish all the information necessary to make a successful gardener of any one who can read, and practice what he learns, but questions continuously arise that cannot be anticipated or answered in a book [catalog] . . . so we publish a Monthly Magazine, in which we answer all these questions."[15] His customers then had an even larger forum for their garden concerns. They would write to Vick and he would regularly include such letters in the pages of the new magazine.

Historians recognize that Vick introduced some of the best methods in mail-order business in order to serve a broad market with great economy.[16] As Charles Birnbaum has noted in the foreword to this book, Vick's business began long before Sears and Montgomery Ward sent out their first catalogs. While seed companies like Robert Buist's in Philadelphia were still illustrating in black ink, Vick was using a chromolithograph on his catalog cover. Both the catalog and the magazine included colored illustrations like the tropical flower called abutilon that appeared in his new monthly in 1879 (fig. 7.3).

Figure 7.3. Abutilon. (*Vick's Monthly Magazine,* 1879.)

8

❧ ❧

Promoting the Seed Business

istorically, the seed business had survived by word of mouth or through plain, unadorned catalogs. Vick used his illustrated cata-log both to promote his seed company and to build a community of lovers of flowers, seeking in any way he could to fill the nation with devotees to floriculture. Through his catalog, and later also through his magazine, Vick promoted the Victorian garden, filled with colorful flowers, as part of a life-style. An illustration in his catalog of 1874, for example, showed a family outside enjoying their fashionable home landscape, including flowers blooming in beds on the lawn (fig. 8.1).

The magazine served to strengthen the link to his customers that the catalogs already had established. One reader wrote, "Mr. Vick: I am so full of the love of flowers that I never get a number of the dear little Magazine without wanting to talk to you a bit."[1]

Vick conducted a business based on his own personal experience and passed on his own love of flowers and of the garden to his customers; he

ae   *Figure 8.1.* "Annual" section in the seed catalog. (*Vick's Floral Guide,* 1874.)

wanted people to treasure a sense of floriculture, whether of outdoor or indoor flowers.

During the late Victorian period, gardeners sought more showy plants for the garden. Canna, cyclamen, and other subtropical plant varieties became essential. Vick wrote in his magazine in 1878, "This class of plants is becoming very popular, and are used in what is known as sub-tropical gardening, that is, gardens furnished with plants of a tropical, or sub-tropical, origin, such as Century Plant, Agaves, Cannas, Caladiums, Ricinus, Yucca, Wigandea, Tritoma, Pampas Grass, etc."[2] One customer wrote to Vick about the ricinus seeds that had come in the mail. She said, "Many thanks for the fine Ricinus seed I got from you last Spring. I have two of the finest specimens of the giant species, 'Giganteus,' one sixteen feet four inches high, and one thirteen feet."[3]

Vick kept up with the latest fashions and trends in gardening, wanting his customers to know about and appreciate plants from various parts of the world, including Asia and South America. Garden historian Edward Hyams writes in his *English Cottage Gardens,* "Plant collectors might have braved the Himalayan and Andean snows in vain, and the work of the plant breeder all *ars gratis artis* had it not been for the coincident growth of a nursery trade to propagate and distribute the new garden plants."[4] This of course holds true for the seed trade as well.

In the second half of the nineteenth century, when ornamental gardening became the fashion, garden writers encouraged their readers to join the tropical plant rage. Using such plants in the garden became a reaction against the bedding-out of annuals with their strong, but flat and monotonous, use of color, usually on the lawn.[5] In early summer, tropical plants were removed from the confines of the greenhouse and planted outside. They occupied beds and vases, and sometimes solitary specimens were placed alone in a container plunged directly into the ground.

❧

Other approaches Vick used to promote floriculture included appearances at state fairs, premium offers, and advertising in newspapers and magazines across the country. His State Street building in downtown Rochester included a store on the first floor. He wrote in his catalog of 1873, "The first floor is used entirely as a sales-shop, or 'store,' for the sale of Seeds, Flowers, Plants and all Garden requisites and adornments, such as baskets, vases, lawn mowers, lawn tents, aquariums, seats, etc. It is arranged with taste, and the songs of the birds, the fragrance and beauty of the flowers, make it a most delightful spot in which to spend an hour" (fig. 8.2).[6]

Figure 8.2. The first-floor interior of Vick's seed store. (Vick's Illustrated Floral Guide, 1873.)

Vick traveled to state fairs to display arrangements of his own flowers. Often, he won awards for such exhibits, as he did at the Wisconsin State Fair in West Allis, outside Milwaukee. His name also appeared in the program for the Pennsylvania State Fair, and in 1872 he took first prize for his dahlias at the New York State Agricultural Society's exhibition.[7] A New York State customer wrote, "I must congratulate you on your fine display of cut flowers at the exhibition of the New York Horticultural Society."[8] The fairs became an opportunity for him to show his customers what his seeds could produce: lovely flowers for the home and garden. He wrote in his magazine, "To encourage the culture of Flowers among the people, and particularly among the people who love them and grow them for love alone, I offer $40.00 in Cash for the Best Show of Flowers at each and every State Fair in America."[9]

He also encouraged his customers to form neighborhood clubs, which would subscribe to both his catalog and his magazine. Requesting help from his readers, Vick wrote, "Many subscribers would do us and their neighbors a favor by getting up a club."[10] Thus, new customers would join his ranks through the influence of local gardeners already receiving his seeds in the mail. He wrote in 1880 that "in this way we have known large clubs to be formed in most unpromising neighborhoods, and a beginning made which, in a few years, entirely changed the appearance of the whole place."[11] The neighborhood of a customer could be reborn through more of its gardeners investing in seeds that would provide colorful flowers at each home. Vick wrote, "We knew the sweet influence of those flowers would be felt as long as time endures."[12]

Vick offered premiums in his catalog as an incentive to those who enlisted new customers to send in orders for his seeds. The premium, or voucher, could be spent for more seeds or one of his chromolithographs of flowers.

Such methods of promoting flowers provided Vick with opportunities to interact with his customers—or his *friends,* as he called them.

❧

Vick also judiciously used advertising as an avenue to spread his message. In the January 1856 issue of *Genesee Farmer,* Vick first advertised his French vegetable and flower seeds, because he "found it impossible to obtain in this country a good article of the finer sorts of seeds."[13] The resulting increase in sales convinced Vick of the important role advertising could play in selling his seeds.

By 1872, the Vick Seed Company was advertising in 3,300 newspapers and in horticultural and agricultural magazines like the *American Agriculturist,* the most popular agricultural magazine at that time (fig. 8.3). With subscribers all over the world, the editor suggested that the name could well be changed to "Cosmopolitan Agriculturalist."[14] An 1881 ad touted, "Vick's seeds are the best in the world. The Floral Guide will tell you how to get and grow them."[15]

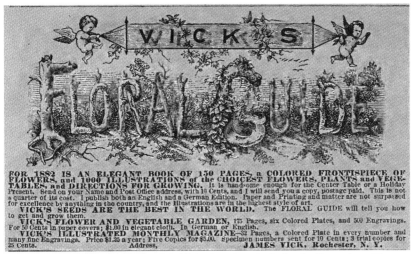

Figure 8.3. Ad for *Vick's Floral Guide* in *American Agriculturist*, December, 1881.

Vick's total advertising bill in December 1870 amounted to $15,000 ($270,000 today), and the bill for stamps came to $4,650 ($92,428 today).[16] Vick took the power of advertising seriously, and had no doubt such ads helped sell his message of flowers to gardeners everywhere. He became a client of J. Walter Thompson, a major Chicago advertising firm. Vick was quoted in one of J. Walter Thompson's own advertisements as attesting, "I have always found the Magazines the very best mediums for advertising my business."[17] *Moore's Rural New Yorker* said of Vick's business, "James Vick is a name fast becoming famous—a household name—among the cultivators and lovers of Flowers all over the land."[18]

But it was, in the end, the catalog that created and sustained Vick's business, and he sought to improve it with every issue. In 1870 he wrote, "I present to my customers and friends my ninth annual catalogue with pleasure, because I think it is not only superior to those previously issued but superior in some respects to any I have ever seen."[19]

Customers' letters provided testimony on how content they were, both with his seeds and with the instructions that he offered for planting and caring for them, and many praised Vick's work in spreading the love of floriculture:

> A customer wrote from Ohio, "Last evening I received your beautiful Monthly Magazine. It was indeed magnificent. I thought I would write and tell you of my wonderful success with flowers."[20]
>
> A gardener from Minnesota said, "Mr. Vick: I feel greatly indebted to you for teaching me how to raise flowers successfully."[21]
>
> A gardener calling herself Terra wrote, "All the ladies sing the praises of the Flower Garden, and half of the men, too, especially the young men, and those to whom the good opinion of the ladies is a matter of great importance."[22]

Vick's reach spanned the globe, and under his leadership, his seed company became one of the largest in the world.[23] His correspondents wrote from far beyond the continental United States, with letters arriving from as far away as China.

People enjoyed the catalog and magazine, reading about floriculture and then cultivating flowers in their own gardens. One customer, Jenny, wrote, "We like the Magazine for several reasons; one is, that it is devoted exclusively to 'the green things growing,' and kindred subjects—it is not a clothes-press nor a cook-shop. Then, it is so practical, and tells us just what we want to know, and so plainly and pleasantly that even a child can comprehend. And last, but not least, it is so beautiful in every respect, and I do think that you are doing a good work in putting so excellent and beautiful a Magazine into the hands of the people at a merely nominal price."[24]

Vick's catalog and his magazine built a community of people who loved flowers and floriculture, and his customers felt a connection to the wider Victorian world of flowers. One customer said, "Mr. Vick: From you I have acquired and put in practice much valuable information concerning the cultivation of flowers."[25]

Vick said, "If you would have the greatest enjoyment from flowers, raise them yourself; plant the seed, tend them with your own hand, watch over them and minister to their wants. In this way to some extent you become identified with them. By their daily growth they respond to your attentions, their bloom is your hope's fruition, their beauty is the realization of your ideal."[26]

❧

Vick wanted to make sure that every family cultivated a flower garden of some kind in the home landscape. Though only a vegetable garden might be seen as essential, according to Vick, where there was limited space the homeowner ought to plant a flower garden first. He said, "While our markets are bountifully supplied with fruits and vegetables at reasonable prices, you can seldom command a neat, fresh bunch of flowers."[27] A taste for the beautiful in gardening, especially a true love of flowers, was available to all. He wrote, "We leave others to write of things which but few can enjoy, while we talk of the beauties within the reach of all, and to be had almost without money or price."[28]

No matter how much money an individual gardener had, the same principles of cultivation applied to each plant, from the commonest weed and most diminutive variety of flower to the tallest tree or the most superb exotic. Nature's rules apply to all plants, whether cultivated by the wealthy, the middle class, or the laborer. Those who had greenhouses and hired gardeners did not need Vick's counsel. He wrote for the millions who did not have such resources, but who nonetheless loved flowers and sought to cultivate them both in the house and in the garden.

❧

Hearing of Vick's death in 1882, Philadelphia nurseryman Thomas Meehan wrote in the June issue of the *Gardeners' Monthly and Horticulturist*, "As we go to press, the telegraph brings news of the death of this distinguished horticulturalist in Rochester, on Tuesday, May 16th, in his sixty-fourth year. The immense influence he has exercised on the great progress of American horticulture is too well known to need any more than a passing note at this time."[29]

At the same time, Celia Thaxter, the late nineteenth-century Maine poet and artist, wrote in one of her letters that she had just learned of his death. Her beautiful garden depended on seeds every year, which she purchased from Vick. He must have seemed to her like an old friend, because she wrote in a letter to her own friend simply, "And now Vick is dead, too."[30]

Although Henderson, Park, Burpee, and Harris were important seedsmen in the final decades of the nineteenth century, James Vick was the most successful horticultural seedsman-writer-merchandiser of that period.[31] The mechanized procedures Vick developed for sorting and packaging his seeds set precedents for modern seed distribution—but it was his writing that inspired and drew his customers.

After his death, Vick's sons took over the company, which continued to dominate the flower and bulb trade in America.[32] They continued the catalog and the magazine into the early 1900s. But it all began with that first Vick catalog in 1861, in which the elder Vick's words spelled out his desire to spread the love of flowers. That goal, coupled with his writing skill, built the company that his sons inherited.

Figure 8.4. Carnations. (*Vick's Monthly Magazine*, 1880.)

9

❧ ❧

Building His Business

The Vick Seed Company grew under its founder's guidance for more than twenty years. He expanded the acreage of the seed test beds. He built a new seed house as his headquarters. He continued to hire more employees. He worked with more editors, artists, and printers.

From his very first catalog in 1861, Vick wanted it to be more than just a listing of seeds for sale. He wanted it to be useful, and he took pride in the precise instructions for planting that the catalog provided for his customers. He was not simply selling a plant; he was also educating a gardener.

The catalog came with a heavy paper cover and generally totaled one hundred fifty pages. Each edition contained several hundred black-and-white engravings, along with at least one and sometimes as many as three or four colored plates.

During the 1860s, Vick conducted his business in the attic of his home, where he filled the seed orders. Since his business was growing and the attic was becoming cramped, he sought out a new location. In 1871, he found a home for the seed company in a four-story building at 60 State Street, on the corner of State and Market Streets in downtown Rochester, where several whole floors were devoted to the business. He shared the news about his company's growth with his customers by providing illustrations of the various departments in the new building (figs. 9.1, 9.2, and 9.3).

Figure 9.1. Order room. (*Vick's Illustrated Floral Guide*, 1873.)

Figure 9.2. Packing room. (*Vick's Illustrated Floral Guide*, 1873.)

ꙮ *Figure 9.3.* Bindery. (*Vick's Illustrated Floral Guide,* 1873.)

Within the walls of his seed house, Vick developed modern, systematic garden seed production and introduced extensive mail order sales to the seed business.[1] By the early 1870s, the railroad linked most American cities, which made shipping seed orders easier and more efficient. It was a time when people had begun to desire standardized products for the home, and mass advertising in newspapers and magazines made such products, including garden seeds, available to a growing middle class. From the beginning, Vick had sought to appeal to this middle-class consumer. Rochester historian W. H. McIntosh wrote in 1877 that "with the establishment of this enterprise [the Vick Seed Company] seeds were placed within the reach of the masses, and a new era was entered upon in the culture of flowers."[2]

The new seed house downtown afforded Vick the space to hire more workers, many seasonal. During the busy season, a staff of more than a hundred was required to contend with the three hundred orders and three thousand letters—many asking questions and hoping for an answer from "Mr. Vick"—that the office received each day. Women were usually employed to open the mail, and other workers filled the orders from storage areas in the upper floors of the building.

From the letters that Vick published in his catalog or the magazine, it would appear that half of his customers were women and young people with no experience in gardening. He was eager to encourage them and to assure some level of success in the garden, no matter how inexperienced they were. He wrote, "My desire to spread the love of flowers all over this favored land is far greater than my care to make a few extra dollars in business."[3]

Vick had his own office, where he wrote and edited both the catalog and his magazine. He wrote an introduction appearing at the front of each catalog, and in the early years he personalized the writings, referring to himself as "I" quite often. In later years, he would sometimes refer to himself and the business as "we." In addition to the business of seeds and plants, he also shared his viewpoints and travels with his readers. In the 1880 issue of the magazine, for example, he described in detail his vacation trip out West to such famous American sites as Yosemite.

❧

As the business continued to grow, within a few years Vick needed an even bigger site for his headquarters. In 1880, on the south side of his home on East Avenue, Vick constructed a four-story brick building near the fifty acres of the "Flower Farm," as he called it (fig. 9.4).

The building had not only offices to process seed orders but also a print shop, bindery, and box-manufacturing facility. Vick also included rooms for his artists, engravers, printers, and binders: "Here we have our artists convenient to our grounds and greenhouses, where they can always procure plants and flowers for drawing and engraving."[4] The Rochester artist John Walton worked for Vick for more than twenty years.[5]

Vick informed his customers about the new seed house in his 1881 seed catalog, writing, "To enable us to better serve our friends and customers,

 Figure 9.4. New Vick seed house in 1880. (*The Industries of the City of Rochester* [Rochester, NY: Elstner, 1888].)

during the last summer we erected on our grounds, on East Avenue, Rochester, N.Y., a large, handsome and convenient building."[6] The new headquarters included flower beds of annuals on the lawn, a garden fashion that Vick often recommended in his magazine. A tall vase filled with blooming annuals stood at the foot of the walkway from the street, illustrating his suggestion to readers regarding the choice of plants to be used in such a container. On the front lawn outside the building, the words "James Vick" appeared, spelled out in flowers in the carpet-bed style, reflecting the popular Victorian garden fashion. Visitors could see his garden advice enacted in the landscape surrounding his own company's building.

The building embodied the latest in design and materials to provide Vick the space and environment he needed. The world could now see how his seed business had grown over the twenty-five years since it had begun.

⁂

Because Vick had been in the publishing business for so many years, he knew a great deal about putting together a catalog and a magazine. His technology of choice for illustrations in both publications was wood engraving, which had been a popular art form commonly used in publishing since the inception of Western printing. It remained the standard until 1881, when line illustrations came into vogue.[7] The process for creating the woodcuts was old and well-established. The artist for the Vick Seed Company used India ink to create a drawing. Then engravers would work up the drawing on wood blocks, which would then be used in printing the drawing on a page for the forthcoming catalog.

Vick felt that his catalog would compare favorably with any literary work in the library, because it was well written and beautifully bound. A customer could take pride in it. The catalog was something to display like any book in the home, since it was an example of the art of a professional bookmaker. One of Vick's customers wrote him after receiving his magazine and said, "Mr. Vick: Allow one of your readers to express thanks for the treat enjoyed upon the reception of the August copy of your Magazine. Its beautiful floral cover is quite a study to begin with, and so arrested the attention upon removing the wrapper that it proved difficult for a time to get any further."[8]

Vick wrote from his own garden experience. You could tell from his writing that there were certain flowers he loved above all others. He spoke of looking at a field of verbenas "more gorgeous than the skill of man ever produced" in the catalog for 1870 (fig. 9.5).[9] He took notes about what he saw in the garden and would provide several details in describing a particular flower.

Charles Seelye, Vick's brother-in-law, served as editor for Vick's publications for many years. Seelye, who had met Vick while on the editorial staff at *Genesee Farmer*, was also a horticulturist, writer, and artist.[10] In 1844, he established the Rochester Central Nurseries with Hiram Sibley. Seelye continued to edit the Vick Company publications long after the senior Vick's death in 1882. He wrote many items for Vick, including the book *How to Lay Out a Lawn*.

᳙

From his testing of seeds, Vick sometimes decided that certain plants were not worthy to appear among the offerings in the catalog. He explained, "Every new or superior variety of seed or seed-producing plants discovered are [*sic*] immediately secured for my own grounds, and every improved practice in growing seeds immediately adopted. No package of seed is allowed to leave my establishment until fairly tested in my trial houses, and if there is any difficulty in germination it is at once condemned."[11] Sometimes it was more a matter of necessity than decision: "Occasionally the crop of a certain variety partially fails, and I only get a small quantity, and sometimes the crop is entirely destroyed, so that I can obtain none, or, in testing, a variety proves worthless, with no time to obtain new stock."[12]

Vick took the role of instructor in his writing seriously. He promised to provide "hints" for everyone in gardening, including the laborer or member of the working class, whom he sometimes called the "intelligent mechanic." He wrote, "The culture of flowers is one of the few pleasures that improves alike the mind and the heart, and makes every true lover of these beautiful creations of Infinite Love wiser and purer and nobler."[13]

Figure 9.5. Verbena. (*Vick's Monthly Magazine,* 1880.)

10

❧ ❧

Vick Lays Out
the Flower Garden

ick's catalog and magazine included instructions on how to set up a garden to grow flowers, whether in beds, borders, or containers, or for cutting. He sometimes laid out a plan or design that a homeowner could easily adapt to suit a particular property, demonstrating how flowers could become an integral feature of the home landscape.

In 1868, when Vick first began offering advice on landscape design, he explained his intention and method: "I have endeavored to give all necessary instructions in a very plain and thorough manner, telling not only *how* work should be done, but stating the reason *why*—giving in a few words the philosophy of the whole matter."[1]

Vick admired the property of his East Avenue neighbor Isaac Butts, editor of the Rochester *Advertiser* and *Union Advertiser* newspapers. Butts's property illustrated the right kind of home landscape, centered on an

Figure 10.1. The Butts residence in Rochester. (*Vick's Monthly Magazine*, 1879.)

extensive lawn and the correct placement of trees. In 1879, Vick included a tree-filled illustration in his magazine that he explained was "of the grounds at the residence of the family of the late Isaac Butts, situated on the south side of East Avenue" (fig. 10.1).[2]

He went on to describe it in appreciative detail, noting that "as there are no front fences in this locality, and even no division fences or hedges, the grounds on this part of the avenue have a beautiful parklike appearance. It will be noticed that the trees are all fine specimens, and this is in a great measure due to the fact, that in planting great care was exercised to allow each tree ample room for its perfect development, and then they have been allowed to assume their natural forms without mutilation by the pruning-knife."[3]

Vick also shared the plan of another property that included flower beds on the lawn (fig. 10.2). The siting of the flower beds is indicated with a *D*. He advised that "the locations of flower-beds . . . should be where the beds could be best seen from the windows of the house, and where they would appear to best advantage from the street."[4]

ᔥᔐ

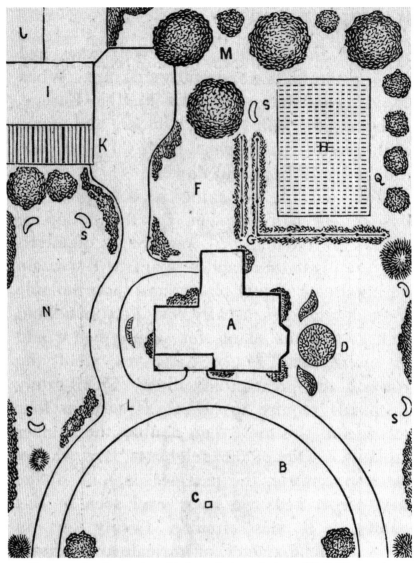

Figure 10.2. Landscape plan with flower beds on the lawn. (*Vick's Illustrated Monthly Magazine*, 1878.)

In 1870, the landscape designer Frank J. Scott wrote *The Art of Beautifying Suburban Home Grounds of Small Extent.* It became an important resource for homeowners intent on learning about landscaping, and the book went through several printings. Nurseries and seed companies like Vick's often recommended it. Philadelphia nursery owner Thomas Meehan reviewed Scott's book in his *Gardeners' Monthly and Horticulturist,* writing, "The preparation of that work commenced as a labor of love. The author went personally over every part of the United States where he could hear of a fine tree, a fine garden, or fine garden architecture, and embodied the work of his pen and pencil in this superb book."[5]

Scott followed the English garden landscape ideals of Andrew Jackson Downing, with whom he spent several months at his home in New York learning about landscape, and he adopted Downing's advice on how to incorporate flowers and flower beds.[6] Vick became familiar with both Downing and Scott through their writing.

Vick followed Scott's recommendation that the homeowner first draw a plan to guide future work on the grounds. Scott argued that if a plan directed the architect and builder in going forward with building a house, and if one would never consider building a house without a plan, why should the homeowner fail to provide the same care in planning for the landscape? Vick, like Scott, was concerned first with mapping out the lawn, walkways, and driveways. Flower beds could later be added to the lawn.

Scott wanted the homeowner to see the lawn from the windows of the house (fig. 10.3). Therefore, its placement required a great deal of attention. Scott said that even if the property were small and located close to other houses on the same street, taking care of the lawn could contribute to a neighbor's enjoyment. Therefore, when designing for a small property, it was important to take into consideration one's view of the neighbor's lawn as well. A neighbor, in turn, would look at an adjoining homeowner's lawn as a part of his view. Thus, the design of a landscape provided a view of an extended lawn both for homeowner and neighbor, especially when the property was small. No wonder homeowners still fret over keeping the lawn mowed.

&e *Figure 10.3.* Home lawn with flower bed. (*Vick's Monthly Magazine,* 1880.)

Adding his own advice to Downing's, Vick wrote that "every touch of art must harmonize with nature; the unity of the place must be preserved." Vick suggested that homeowners familiarize themselves with what the property had to offer in terms of natural slopes and contours, existing plants, shade, and water. "First, then, study the place; go often to it and place yourself in communion with it. . . . When you have gained this, you have the key that, skilfully used, will solve all the problems connected with the work." He further advised, "Do not mar what is already beautiful. If you should heighten an effect or add a grace you will do well, but be careful that you do not introduce some incongruous feature."[7]

Only after the homeowner had studied the place was it time to draw a plan for the landscape. Vick noted that his readers would not be able to take a particular plan from either his catalog or his magazine and apply it mechanically to their own property. Nonetheless, they could learn from such a plan how to apply the general principles of landscape gardening with flowers.

A landscape plan could be simple or elaborate, depending on the skills of the designer and space that he or she had to work with. Though landscape architecture would not become a profession in America until nearly the twentieth century, competent gardeners, engineers, and architects throughout the nineteenth century produced plans to provide guidance for the design of the home landscape. Flowers, whether in beds or borders, would usually be an integral part of such a plan.

In the 1870s and 1880s, Elias Long, a popular landscape designer from Buffalo, New York, advised that a plan should deliberately site any flowers and avoid simply dotting the lawn with flower beds, writing, "In the use of seed-grown plants in such places [as a home garden], or in any place, if the massing plan were more generally observed in setting them, these flowers would have a better reputation in fine gardens."[8] Thus, Long proposed a mass planting of the same variety of flowers in a bed, arguing that it would provide a strong visual impact for the landscape.

Vick recognized that the homeowner might hire a landscape designer like Long to provide a plan, but that plan still had to follow the desires and wishes of the homeowner. As if echoing Vick's idea, the late-nineteenth-century American landscape architect Ossian Cole Simonds wrote, "While the landscape-gardener may make the original design, in its most perfect form it must be developed, adopted, and loved by its owner."[9]

No matter what style of design a homeowner might prefer, Vick still emphasized the importance of having a plan. It was much easier to look at the landscape on paper and to move plants, make changes, and insert additions on a plan than it was to make changes later with plants already in the ground.

❧

The plan therefore ought to illustrate flower beds on the lawn, usually planted in carpet-bed style, perhaps round or diamond-shaped in the prevailing Victorian fashion of the day (fig. 10.4). Scott included such flower beds in his drawings of plans in his book. Vick wrote, "Instead of flowers a few weeks in the year, as in the olden time, there are now unbroken beds of beauty from early spring until the frost-king lays his cold hand upon every leaf and flower."[10]

The beds ought to include flowers that would bloom for the entire season. Therefore, Vick preferred annuals. He wrote, "A few flower beds may be made, and usually near the borders, or opposite windows, and they should be of simple, graceful forms, and look well the whole summer, and every day and all day."[11]

Vick's plans sometimes specified the varieties of flowers to be planted, but it was the inclusion and design of the beds themselves that was integral to the homeowner's plan, regardless of which species eventually was selected. Such a form of gardening had become essential in the late Victorian landscape.

Vick cautioned about too much planting in the landscape. He said that two great errors were usually made, both by seasoned gardeners and amateurs: one destroying the lawn by cutting it up with unnecessary walks and flower beds, the other producing the same result by almost literally covering it with trees and shrubbery. The location of flower beds on the lawn, whether annuals or perennials, might vary, but it remained important that the beds be positioned so they could be best seen from the windows of the house, and where they would appear in all their glory from the street (fig. 10.5).

In another popular garden fashion, flowers could be the same height and color and planted in rows, giving the appearance of stripes in ribbons.[12] That Victorian garden style became known as ribbon beds. Flower beds on the lawn were there to be enjoyed by the homeowner and visitors. Cutting flowers from them was not encouraged: "no presents for friends, no bouquet for the dining room, or for schools or churches, or the sick room."[13] Out of view of visitors, a cutting garden ought to be planted behind the house for such purposes.

According to Vick, cultivating flowers contributed to the health of the family. "The change has done much to make people better, healthier and happier; but its happiest effects are with the women and children, affording healthful recreation and ennobling amusement. Some of the men, we fear, are enjoying blessings they neither appreciate nor deserve. We have heard of a few rare cases left of men who try to show their manhood by contempt of

Figure 10.4. Flower bed with ricinus, canna, and caladium. (*Vick's Monthly Magazine,* 1880.)

Figure 10.5. Perennial garden. (*Vick's Illustrated Catalogue and Floral Guide,* 1870.)

beauty. They are, however, remnants of a race almost extinct. Men of brains are helpers in the good work, and nobly aid the weaker and wiser ones in making homes of beauty."[14]

Vick was not alone in his opinion that women could and should partake in flower gardening. In 1869, when American abolitionist and author Harriet Beecher Stowe and her sister wrote their book about the woman's role in making an economical, healthful, beautiful, and Christian home, they included a section about such flower beds on the lawn. They wrote, "In yards which are covered with turf, beds can be cut out of it, and raised for flowers. A trench should be made around, to prevent the grass from running on them."[15]

For an example of how flower beds could improve a property, Vick presented the case of an area around a schoolhouse in need of landscaping. In addition to enjoying a beautiful and healthful environment, children could learn about flowers and also come to appreciate the works of nature (figs. 10.6 and 10.7). Notice the tall ricinus, or castor oil plant, one of Vick's favorites, planted at the far left in the center of the back flower bed.

Figure 10.6. School house before flowers. (*Vick's Monthly Magazine,* 1880.)

Figure 10.7. School house after planting flowers. (*Vick's Monthly Magazine,* 1880.)

Teachers often wrote to him for help with improving the grounds that surrounded their schools. They sometimes would buy seeds from Vick and in turn offer them to their students. Students sometimes also received prizes for their success with growing the seeds. Vick even offered a year's subscription to his magazine as a prize. Vick's relationship with teachers provided him an opportunity to spread his love of flowers to the next generation of gardeners. Vick predicted that children who enjoyed something as simple as a flower bed on the school property would be inspired to garden throughout their lives. He wrote, "Children will learn all the better with these fair things about them, and acquire a taste and refinement which will sweeten and beautify all their lives, the result of which, in the great future, no philosopher is wise enough to tell."[16]

❧

Where there was an extensive lawn in the garden plan, Vick encouraged that a large, well-filled vase be placed in the center of each side of the lawn. Tall flowers and plants with ornamental foliage were best for such a vase (fig. 10.8), and he provided guidelines for the choice of plants and their care. He wanted the reader to know the protocol for such containers in the landscape. Vick wrote, "The finest ornament of the lawn is the vase, and it is better to have one or two that command attention by their size and gratify the taste by their beauty than a dozen small ones scattered over the lawn."[17]

The container, vase, or urn could be made of cast iron, a material more affordable for the middle-class gardener. Vases of marble or granite were too costly for general use. Many vases, however, in equally beautiful forms, were also manufactured of artificial stone or fine pottery as well as cast iron, which gave the same effect and were of nearly equal durability as more expensive garden decorations.[18] The vase was to sit on a pedestal and not directly on the lawn. Thus, more people could see it. The recommended number of vases to be displayed was two, to be positioned on either side of the front entrance to the house.

❧ *Figure 10.8.* A vase on the lawn. (*Vick's Monthly Magazine,* 1879.)

Vick wrote, "Nothing is more effective than a well filled and well kept vase."[19] He prescribed that this vase be "a well-cared-for container" and bemoaned the fact that slipshod gardeners sometimes neglected these vessels, so that during the hot summer months the plants dried up for lack of attention. In 1874, he wrote, "Last year we published an article on the proper treatment of Baskets and Vases, showing that many failed simply because the plants were famished, destroyed entirely, or condemned to a miserable struggle for existence simply for want of water."[20]

Vick also provided specific instructions on the variety of plants to include in an outdoor vase. He advised a tall, showy plant in the center like a yucca or canna. A shorter plant, such as a verbena or petunia, was to fill out the midsection. Finally, a hanging plant like an ivy or coleus ought to droop down the side of the container. That hanging plant was never, of course, to touch the ground, and the homeowner was advised to keep it well trimmed. Each of these recommended flowers numbered among Vick's most treasured.

𝕾𝕰

After 1850, flower arranging took hold as an art form and passion, and seed and nursery catalogs moved from selling mostly vegetables to include more flowers. Gardeners wanted flowers, and the seed companies moved to keep up with that demand.[21] The decoration of rooms with cut flowers became increasingly important and gave rise by midcentury to all sorts of containers to hold flowers and keep them fresh. Vick offered many flower suggestions in the back pages of his seed catalog, including wooden, metal, and ceramic vases.

The Victorian home demanded flower arrangements for many occasions, and because women generally were expected to provide them, they often turned to experts like Vick for advice.[22] For the cutting garden, Vick suggested annuals like asters, balsams, zinnias, and mignonette. He also recommended that the bed should be four or five feet wide, so one could reach halfway across, and should also include a path or alley to make weeding the bed that much easier. Vick wrote, "Nothing can equal bright, fresh flowers for the adornment of the sacred home, or the still more sacred house of worship. Flowers are grateful every day, and particularly so on special occasions, either of sadness or joy. Once they were costly luxuries, attainable only by the wealthy; now they are a necessity in almost every household."[23]

The Victorians not only loved flower arranging but they passed the tradition on so well that today we still choose many of the same blossoms for our own arrangements. Not long ago in London, contemporary English florist Vic Brotherson designed the flower arrangements for model Kate Moss's wedding. The flowers Brotherson chose included Victorian favorites like foxglove, allium, cosmos, roses, and dahlias.[24]

Plants with attractive leaves, like the canna, ricinus, amaranth, or perilla, also could be used in the flower bed in groups of a half dozen or more. Vick wrote, "A few beds of foliage plants or flowers, or vases, are like diamonds set in emerald, and the latter, especially, impart a graceful elegance which nothing else can give."[25]

Whether in flower beds, borders, containers, or a cutting garden, flowers had to be part of the landscape. The placement of the flowers, however, depended on the landscape plan, which was prepared before any work on the home grounds began. Vick not only sold flower seeds but also provided his readers with instructions on how to benefit from them in the garden. An Illinois reader summed up many others' feelings about Vick's advice, "I will only say, plant flowers, nurse them, give them away freely, love them for the giver's sake, thank God and Vick, and be happy."[26]

11

Vick Sells the Same
Flowers Year after Year

nce in late May I was visiting the Amalfi coast in Italy. It was a beautiful place, where I saw cannas growing in raised beds in the middle of a main street. These showy Victorian plant favorites come up every spring and offer their beautiful, bold flowers for the hot summer days along the Mediterranean. There is no need to dig up the tubers to store them through the winter, as we do here in America's Northeast, since winter temperatures in Amalfi remain mild.

One morning we boarded a boat to the nearby Isle of Capri. Everybody wants to see Capri. We were given a couple of hours to walk around and visit the shops and sights of the island. While we waited for the boat to return to Amalfi, I took a seat on the dock. Not far away I noticed a small garden center, selling plants that were displayed along the sidewalk outside. I walked over to see them.

To my surprise, the plants were annuals that every garden center here in the United States also sells at about the same time of year, early to late spring. The selection included geraniums, petunias, marigolds, impatiens, and alyssum. I was familiar with these plants, ideal for outdoor summer containers and flower beds.

I thought how strange it was that Italian garden centers sold the same annuals that we sell here in the States. These annuals have been part of the American gardener's palette for decades. The seed industry of the late nineteenth century, as embodied in James Vick, created the choice of flowers sold for today's garden. We still garden with the same flowers sold to us in Victorian America.

In ornamental horticulture, the important thing is novelty—something to keep the customers coming back year after year. The plant, however, cannot be too new. Gardeners, both professional and amateur, feel safe sticking to a limited number of plant genera.[1] That is exactly what has happened in the garden industry since the late nineteenth century, when the production and marketing of seeds and plants, like many other industries of that time, entered the big-business arena. The same annuals Vick sold in Victorian America still appear on the market. Gardeners still buy them today.

Though he often introduced new cultivars or varieties, Vick sold the same annuals we still plant today, including warhorses like the petunia, geranium, verbena, alyssum, phlox, and impatiens. Customers kept coming back to Vick for the same plants year after year, including the sweet pea (fig. 11.1).

The most important feature of the annual is that its flowers blossom continuously for the entire growing season. Sometimes you may have to remove dead flowers, but you can depend on annuals to provide an ongoing color in a container, border, or bed.

An annual can be started from seed, or a gardener can purchase small plants in spring—an option that saves the gardener that initial work of planting the seeds and caring for them as they emerge and grow over several

weeks. Vick frequently wrote about the factors important in successfully planting seeds of annual plants: good soil, light, and watering.

To please his customers, Vick was always in search of improved varieties of his popular annuals. In 1865, he called himself an "Importer of Choice Flower and Vegetable Seeds." He received seeds from growers both in the United States and in Europe, but he tested the seeds before he sent them out.[2] He was careful about including novelties, some of which would never become regular items for sale in his catalog. His testing procedures allowed him to identify the poor quality and flaws.

There were certain flowers that Vick preferred, like the petunia (fig. 11.2). The nineteenth-century English garden maven William Robinson wrote in his magazine, *The Garden,* "The tendency now-a-days with most subjects is to get the flowers as large as possible, and the Petunia is no exception to the rule."[3]

Vick first saw petunias in 1826 in England. At that time, he called the flower from South America "strange." The flower was small and white, and, with its delicate appearance, looked as if it were made of paper. A few years later, in 1831, a new petunia, purple in color, arrived in England from Buenos Aires. The new petunia flowered in the Botanic Gardens of Glasgow. Its seed was sent all over Europe, as well as to America.

By 1845, the petunia appeared in the seed catalog of Boston florist Joseph Breck. The colors of the flower were white, purple, and mixed. In the catalog, the petunia varieties were called *nyctaginiflora, phoenicea,* and *var.*

Twenty years later, when he began his business, Vick included the petunia in his catalog. He wrote, "No flower ever became a greater favorite in so short a time, and few have maintained merited popularity so long."[4]

The petunia, as Vick wrote, was divided into three classes: grandiflora, small flowered, and double. The grandiflora bore seeds, but only through a process of hybridizing. The double petunia gave no seed, so this variety also had to be hybridized. Seeds from the small flowered petunia were obtained by crossing single flowers with the pollen of the double.

🙠 *Figure 11.1.* Sweet pea. (*Vick's Magazine,* 1882.)

Cornell University horticulturist Liberty Bailey wrote that "double forms [of petunias] are produced by crossing the most double flowers that are capable of producing good pollen on the best single strains."[5] Vick used that method in his own petunia hybridizing in the early 1870s. Vick set aside a room in his greenhouse that he filled with single-flowering plants, while nearby he filled another room with plants bearing double flowers (fig. 11.3).

❦ Figure 11.2. (facing page) Petunia. (Vick's Monthly Magazine, 1879.)

❦ Figure 11.3. Hybridizing petunias at Vick's flower farm. (Vick's Monthly Magazine, 1879.)

☾ *Figure 11.4.* Crossing single petunias with pollen from double flowers at Vick's flower farm. (*Vick's Monthly Magazine,* 1879.)

A basket filled with double-flowered plants was taken to the area containing single petunias. The double flowers were shredded in search of pollen and the pollen collected with a camel-hair brush. This pollen was then transferred to the pistils of the single flowers (fig. 11.4).

This was an expensive way to generate seeds, but it was from this method that Vick developed his own petunia cultivar, 'Vick's New Fringed,' in 1871. In the 1865 edition of his seed catalog, Vick had offered eight petunia seed varieties. That same group of seeds remained for sale until the early 1880s, when four more varieties were added, including the 'Vick's New Fringed.'

In Vick's method of hybridizing, double flowers occurred in only 20 to 30 percent of the plants grown from seed; the rest would be large singles. It took until the twentieth century for hybridizers to bring the genetics of Mendel to bear on petunia plant breeding.[6]

Though extensive hybridizing of shrubs like roses and rhododendron, perennials like the iris and the delphinium, along with annuals like the geranium and verbena, took place in the nineteenth century, it was only after 1900 that plant selection and breeding became a systematic science.[7] That science has given the garden world several cultivars of the petunia, including the striped petunia (*Petunia* x *hybrida*).

❧

It was no surprise that the petunia became one of the most popular annuals in Victorian America. Peter Henderson, in his 1883 book *Gardening for Pleasure*, gives a list of important annuals, among which he included the petunia.

A gardener from Washington wrote to Vick, "I have succeeded splendidly with Asters, Petunias, Portulaca, Phlox, Stock, Verbena, Larkspurs, Pansies, Antirrhinum, and, in fact, all the hardy annuals."[8] Another reader sent along her list of the twelve best annuals. It included pansy, dianthus, stock, *Phlox drummondii*, petunia, balsam, sweet pea, aster, alyssum, mignonette, and verbena.[9]

A customer once asked Vick to name what he considered the best six annuals. Vick responded, "We hardly know what to recommend for six best Annuals; or, rather, we shall have to omit some that we would like to include in every list." He proceeded to name five—phlox, striped petunia, double portulaca, pansy, aster. Then he named six more, none of which he could include in his list because it would mean excluding the others, and ended by saying, "so our readers had better select the last one for themselves, for we can't find it in our heart to exclude so many good things from our list of six, and perhaps make hard feelings among our favorite flowers. We speak of all that bloom the first season as annuals."[10]

In the late nineteenth century, Vick, like so many other hybridizers who were seed company or nursery owners, was breeding the same plants that had been popular for decades. According to garden historian Richard Gorer, "The hybridists appear to have gone on breeding the same plants so long . . . they seem to lack enterprise."[11] Why didn't they hybridize other plant species and their cultivars? Perhaps their choice was based more on what would sell. A gardener would be more likely to choose a new version of a familiar plant than a completely unfamiliar new plant. There was a feeling of reliability that came with the old, established line of garden favorites. We still plant the same annuals that Vick offered for sale in his seed catalog of the nineteenth century. New versions of familiar plants continue to sell well.

Vick also worked to improve the popular annual aster (fig. 11.5). By the 1880s, seedsmen, obviously eager to produce their own lines of flower seed, offered named aster cultivars, as with the 'Vick's Branching' China aster.[12]

Of the geranium, a reader wrote to Vick, "There is probably no flower more generally cultivated in America than the Geranium. . . . Much has been done by florists during the past few years to improve this plant, and their efforts have been crowned with success. We have now so long a list of varieties desirable for beauty of form and color that one might well hesitate when attempting to select specimens."[13] Hybridizing the popular geranium proved a success also for Vick.

Today the number-one-selling annual is the calibrachoa, or "Million Bells," which is in the family Solanaceae like the petunia. Not far behind it in popularity you will find the new petunia hybrid that every gardener wants today, Supertunia. The grower Proven Winners's number-one annual for the last year was the Supertunia 'Royal Velvet.'

Figure 11.5. Asters. (*Vick's Monthly Magazine*, 1882.)

It was the familiar annuals I saw in Italy that made me think how big, yet how limited at the same time, the plant industry had become. It is now based on an international market for gardeners who are offered the same plants across the world.

Figure 11.6. Annuals. (*Vick's Flower and Vegetable Garden*, 1875.)

12

❧ ❧

Victorian Flowers
That Vick Loved

n both his seed catalog and his magazine, it was clear that Vick preferred some flowers over others. The following is a list of fifty flowers
that Vick wrote about often, most of them annuals. Included in the list are
a few plants that, though not known for their flowers, were still an integral
part of Victorian gardening, like the caladium, coleus, and perilla, all of
which were cultivated for their colorful leaves. The list also includes a few
perennials, along with some tender bulbs or tubers like the begonia, which
just shines in the summer garden (fig. 12.1).

In his catalog, under the illustration of a flower, Vick often described its
particular value. His love for each genus or variety came across as he sought
to convey their importance in the garden and to share with the homeowner
what he personally found to be enjoyable and meaningful. Vick's writing
about each of them contributed to their status as "must have" plants to this
very day.

 Figure 12.1. Begonias. (*Vick's Monthly Magazine,* 1879.)

The following list of flowers became popular in part because, like James Vick, many other seed company owners wrote about them, promoted them, praised them, featured them, and spoke about their importance and worthiness in the garden. Their words not only communicated a message, but they created a world in which each variety of flower played its own prominent role. That these flowers remain important for gardeners to this day highlights the value of Vick's writing and that of his contemporaries.[1]

In 1876, Vick compiled several of his articles and descriptions of plants from his catalogs in a book called *Vick's Flower and Vegetable Garden.* Each description below is in Vick's own words from either that book, his catalog *Vick's Floral Guide* (1880), or his magazine *Vick's Illustrated Monthly,* starting from the issue of March 1879.

❧

Alyssum. The Sweet Alyssum has pretty little white flowers, useful in making up all kinds of small bouquets; and its fragrance, while sufficiently pronounced, is very delicate, reminding one of the peculiar aroma of the hay field.

Amaranthus. The genus *Amaranthus* embraces a large class of plants, mainly valuable for their ornamental foliage, the leaves of most varieties being highly colored, while in some the form as well as the color is desirable.

Anemone japonica 'Alba.' One of the best hardy, white-blooming, autumn-flowering plants we have.

Aquilegia. A very showy and in every way interesting and beautiful genus of hardy perennials. Flowers curious and fine; colors varied and striking. . . . A bed of fine *Aquilegias,* when in flower, is not excelled.

Aster. The Aster was popular when we had our little garden nearly half a century ago. We used to call it then China Aster, but those children who wished to be very nice would say *Reine Marguerite,* and would often get laughed at for preferring so hard a name, just because it was French. The Aster was sent to France from China by a Missionary, and the English name means *China Star,* while the French is *Queen Daisy.*

Balsam. Like the Aster, . . . one of the most beautiful and popular of our Annuals. Like that flower, too, it is an old favorite, and so much improved during the last quarter of a century, that it scarcely bears a resemblance to the old flower. . . . Our climate is wonderfully adapted to the growth of the Balsam.

Begonia. The tuberous-rooted Begonias are becoming quite popular for planting out in the spring. . . . The bulbs are of singular appearance, and produce fine plants that will flower profusely until frost, either in the garden or in pots, and seem to bear either sun or shade.

Calendula. The Calendula is the fine old and well known Marigold family, which everyone knows, but may not recognize by this name. Single varieties are not so much cultivated as the double.

Calla. This is the well known Egyptian Lily, or Lily of the Nile, with large white flowers, broad foliage, and it will prosper under very adverse circumstances. . . . In the spring they may be planted in the garden, and should not be encouraged to grow, but rather let them remain in a partial dormant state until autumn.

Caladium. The Caladium esculentum is one of the handsomest of the ornamental-leaved plants. Roots obtained in the spring will make good plants in the summer, and in the fall they should be taken up and stored in a cellar.

Candytuft. One of the oldest and most popular and useful little flowers is the Candytuft. It blooms long and freely, is perfectly hardy, so that most kinds may be sown in the earliest spring, or even in the autumn. Its neat little clusters of flowers are quite a treasure to the bouquet maker, particularly the white.

Canna. The Cannas are stately plants, with broad, green, highly ornamental leaves. . . . There are several varieties, the leaves of some being entirely green, while in others the leaf-stem, mid-rib and veins are red. Some kinds grow four to five feet in height, while others are only about three feet.

Carnations. The most magnificent of all the Dianthus family. Flowers large, beautiful, and delightfully fragrant; a rival of the Rose.

Celosia. There are two desirable forms of the Celosia, the *Cockscomb* and the *Feathered.* . . . Seed can now be obtained that, with good culture, in a rich soil, will give heads of six inches to a foot across.

Chrysanthemum. The prettiest of late autumn and early winter flowering plants. In November and December there is nothing that will make such a cheerful display.

Coleus. The Coleus are the best and cheapest ornamental leaved plants we have for ornamental bedding, in what is sometimes called the carpet style. A few dozens of these plants will make a bed of which no one will have any cause to be ashamed.

Convolvulus major. The old Morning Glory . . . is the best known and most popular, and all things considered, perhaps, the best Annual Climber we have. The seeds germinate so readily that they can be grown in the garden in any corner where the plants are needed (fig. 12.2).

ⅇ *Figure 12.2. Morning glory. (Vick's Monthly Magazine,* 1880.)

Dahlia. The Dahlia is the grandest Autumn flower we have. Nothing is its equal in any respect in September and October. It is in its glory when everything else is faded or fading, and surrenders only to the Frost King.

Datura. Datura is a large, strong-growing plant, with trumpet-shaped flowers, the best bearing blooms six inches in length, mostly white, sometimes tinted with a delicate blue.

Dianthus. The varieties of Dianthus known as Chinese Pinks and Japan Pinks are among the most brilliant of our garden flowers. Plants of the tall sorts are from twelve to fifteen inches in height; the dwarf make low, compact plants.

Gaillardia. Gaillardia, known as Blanket Flowers, are good bedding annuals, being strong, constant bloomers through the whole summer (fig. 12.3).

Geranium. No flower is more generally and successfully cultivated than the *Geranium.* It is found in almost every garden and in every house where plants are cultivated, in every part of the civilized world. It is so easily grown, either from seeds or cuttings, . . . that it must always be a special favorite with those who cultivate house plants.

Gladiolus. The Gladiolus is the most beautiful of our Summer Bulbs, with tall spikes of flowers, some two feet or more in height, and often several spikes from the same bulb. The flowers are of almost every desirable color—brilliant scarlet, crimson, creamy white, striped, blotched and spotted in the most curious and interesting manner.

Heliotrope. This plant is a universal favorite. It was originally brought from Peru, and thus received its name *H. Peruvianum.* It is a small, branching, shrubby plant, growing from three to five feet high.

Hollyhock. In situations suitable for tall flowers, we know of nothing better than the Hollyhock. . . . A good, double, clear, white Hollyhock is a very good substitute for a Camellia or a white Rose, as a center of a bouquet.

Hyacinth. The most popular, as also the most beautiful and fragrant of the bulbous flowers. . . . It seems particularly adapted to house culture.

Iris. The Iris, or Flowering Flag, as it is called, or *Fleur de lis* of the French, is a well known family of hardy border flowers. They are natives of damp spots in all four quarters of the globe, but were adopted for garden culture more than three hundred years ago.

Figure 12.3. Gaillardia. (*Vick's Monthly Magazine*, 1882.)

Lilies. With few exceptions, Lilies succeed in our gardens admirably, and continue to increase in strength and beauty for many years. The collection of Lilies is now so large and so good that no lover of flowers can afford to ignore this interesting and elegant family, and no garden can be considered complete without a good collection.

Lily of the Valley. As hardy as any plant can possibly be, and when planted in the open ground will increase pretty rapidly.

Lobelia. Some of the Lobelias are hardy perennials, like the Cardinal Flower. Annual varieties are mostly of a trailing habit, bearing numbers of small flowers, fine for baskets, vases, edges of beds, etc.

Lychnis. To obtain good flowers the first summer, start seeds under glass and transplant as early as the weather will permit. . . . The flowers are of a great variety of colors, such as rose, red, white, scarlet, etc.

Mignonette. Seeds of Mignonette can be sown at any season, so that by having pots prepared at different times a succession of flowers can be secured, and Mignonette adorn the button hole, and perfume the house at all times.

Narcissus. A very fine class of early blooming flowers, including the well known Daffodil and Jonquil.

Oxalis. One of the prettiest plants we are acquainted with for borders of beds, edging of walks, etc. It forms a rounded edging less than a foot in height, and about the same in breadth.

Pansy. A popular flower with both florists and amateurs, giving abundance of bloom until after severe frosts, enduring our hard winters with safety, and greeting us in the earliest spring with a profusion of bright blossoms.

Perilla. One of the best of the ornamental-leaved annuals. It has a broad, serrated leaf, of a purplish mulberry color, and eighteen inches or more in height.

Petunia. Petunia seed sown in the spring will produce flowering plants in June. . . . They come pretty true from seed, but are not reliable in this respect, being inclined to sport.

Phlox. The flowers of the perennial Phlox, when the plants get strong, are immense bunches of bloom, from the purest white to crimson.

Pink. Very closely related to the Picotee and Carnation, but smaller flowers and more hardy. Flowers very beautiful and fragrant. . . . Treatment same as Carnation.

Ranunculus. Not considered hardy generally, but with good dry soil, with drainage so that the surface water may run off easily, tolerable success may be obtained. Desirable for culture in the house.

Ricinus. Very ornamental foliage and showy fruit.

Rose. No garden, however small, is complete without Roses. The Rose stands, as it has for years, Queen of the Flowers. With a proper selection of kinds, we can have our Roses from June till heavy frosts come with withering touch.

Scabiosa. The tall Scabiosas grow eighteen inches in height, the flowers being on long, wiry stems.

Scilla. The brightest and prettiest and hardiest of the early spring flowers. When the Crocuses are in bloom the little modest *S. siberica* and *S. companulata* may be seen throwing up a little cluster of flowers of the most intense blue imaginable.

Snow-Drop. The first flower of spring is the delicate Snow-Drop, white as snow. Its appearance, about the first of March, is a joyful surprise.

Thunbergia. Thunbergia starts rather slowly at first. . . . Flowers white or orange; fine for baskets.

Tulip. So perfectly hardy, flourishes so well under the most ordinary care, and is so varied and brilliant, that it never fails to give the greatest satisfaction. I sell but very few bulbs with so much pleasure as the Tulips, because I feel sure they will be more than satisfactory (fig. 12.4).

Verbena. Sow Verbena seed under glass early in the spring, and transplant after three or four inches of growth.

Violets. The little, sweet-scented, Double Violet is perfectly hardy, and flowers freely very early in the spring.

Zinnia. A large, free-growing flower, so easily grown, and so handsome that it will always be popular. It is in flower all summer.

Figure 12.4. Tulips. (*Vick's Monthly Magazine*, 1879.)

13

❧ ❧

Vick's Success

We Still Love His Victorian Flowers

oday we take the growing of flowers in a garden as a custom that must have been around forever. That is not the case. It was only when the cultural attitude toward flowers changed that they emerged as essential for both medicine and personal and home decoration.

For much of history, agriculture or practical gardening ruled, and most common people considered flower gardens a vain expenditure of land and labor. The slow shift to pleasure gardening over centuries of change is at the heart of James Vick's story. His life and career illustrate the changes that had come to the world of gardening by the 1800s.

The culture of flowers put down deep roots in most early societies of the Mediterranean and the Near East.[1] Greece and Rome, whose cultures dominated the West and Middle East for centuries, held flowers in high esteem. The majority of Greek and Roman gardening, however, was practical, focusing on foods, medicines, scents, and dyes. Pleasure gardens with flowers appeared mostly in and around palaces and temples. Leaves and flowers were grown for wreaths, ointments, and displays of honor and virtue. The Greeks and Romans not only grew flowers in elaborate gardens in villas and country homes, but they created images of them in various art forms.

The city of Pompeii, a colony of Rome, knew and appreciated horticulture quite early, using flowers for garlands and perfume.[2]

The Middle Eastern peoples treasured closed gardens, often a mix of herbal plants and flowers for pleasure. The powerful image of the garden is woven into Middle Eastern religion. At some points in history, Judaism, Christianity, and Islam developed traditions against iconic images that limited the depiction of flowers because of a perceived link to idolatry, but all three also have the image of Eden at their heart.

Early monasteries of Europe, like that of Saint Benedict, founded in the sixth century, included walled gardens. The monasteries cultivated flowers for religious decoration and for their medicinal and culinary properties. The monastic system was part of a slow process of growing appreciation for horticulture that covered some thousand years.[3]

The Benedictine nun Hildegard von Bingen (1098–1179) encouraged a natural well-being of body and mind. She grew herbs and flowers in the garden to provide for such needs for both her monastery and the nearby villagers who sought her form of healing.

Flowers were also cultivated in medieval towns and villages. By the 1350s, cottage gardeners were gathering their flowers and herbs from the countryside, but they also took seeds and plants offered by the monastery garden.[4]

It took the Enlightenment and the Renaissance to return true pleasure gardens to culture—if still only maintained by the wealthy and powerful. The Renaissance returned to many of the cultural assumptions of Greece and Rome to European culture. Meanwhile, technical and financial advances brought wealth, security, stability, and new agricultural methods that made pleasure gardening a luxury within reach of the upper classes. The spread of wealth and knowledge during the Enlightenment then opened up the dream of pleasure gardens to a landed gentry and mercantile class.

The Renaissance encouraged two main sources of influence on the garden. First, an emphasis on humanistic thought, which aroused interest in old Roman traditions, like a return to Virgil's *Georgics,* his poem on agriculture. This period also saw an awakening of appreciation of the beauties of nature. In the sixteenth century, in both Catholic and Protestant countries, flowers accompanied a renewed interest by artists in the Roman goddess Flora. She appeared in the artwork of Rubens, Rembrandt, and Poussin.

From Italy the Renaissance interest in nature and flowers spread to France, Germany, Spain, Holland, and England, but during the sixteenth-century religious reformation, the cottage gardener lost the figure who had for centuries been his friend, mentor, and teacher: the monastery gardener.[5]

The number of flower choices that appeared in English gardens increased from the eighteenth to the nineteenth century, especially because of botanist explorers. At the same time, there were a number of familiar plant varieties that remained consistently popular. English botanist Philip Miller included annual flowers in his 1731 book *The Gardener's Dictionary.* Many of the same flowers also appeared in Jane Loudon's *Ladies' Companion to the Flower Garden* in 1841. In his *Handy Book of the Flower-Garden,* first appearing in 1863, David Thomson, editor of the British magazine *The Gardener,* included the same plants as well as some newer varieties.

Through the advice of the seed catalog, Americans, too, planted many of the same flowers as the English. Vick's catalog included them along with newer introductions, like the best of the ever-changing number of hybrids on the market. Many of his flowers, however, share a long tradition, as varieties that grew in the English garden.

❧

By the mid-nineteenth century in America, flowers had become part of the garden for every class in society. Cottage gardeners taught by example the art of making good use of a small place.[6] The English magazine *Cottage Gardener* first appeared in 1848. Around the same time, garden catalogs in England and America began to appear in greater numbers, offering seeds that anyone could grow in any size garden.

Such a culture, where flowers played a key role, could not help but embrace a figure like James Vick with open arms. In the early 1860s, Vick was tapping into and at the same time creating the culture's view of the importance of flowers for the garden.

In this atmosphere of desire to learn about floriculture, Vick and his customers formed a common bond. He became the spokesperson for Victorian floriculture in the United States. People loved him and sought out his business because they wanted what he had to offer: seeds of flowers that had long been a part of the garden as well the most current and important varieties. He gave generously of his experience and his knowledge of flowers.

When asked to name his favorite annuals, Vick listed plants familiar to gardeners today. Not much has changed in the choice of annuals for the home gardener except a greater number of cultivars. The variety of plant species attractive to the home gardener remains basically the same.

Today it is no surprise that when you enter a box store or any garden center in the spring, you see familiar annuals that were also sold in the nineteenth century, when flower gardening became popular with the middle class and access to seeds and plants increased through mass production, packaging, and shipping. The box stores Lowe's and Home Depot offer the same annuals for sale. The top ten annuals featured at Lowe's include alyssum, amaranth, angelonia, begonia, celosia, euphorbia, heliotrope, marigold, salvia, and zinnia. Home Depot's most popular annuals include petunia, impatiens, geranium, and begonia. Every year, Proven Winners, one of the country's largest growers for the home gardener, produces a list of its top fifty annuals, and the first ten often include such familiar plants as Supertunia, calibrachoa, bacopa, euphorbia, and lobelia.[7]

Every year, a research center at the University of Minnesota conducts summer trials of hundreds of annuals and provides a similar list of the ten top-performing plants, along with a report on all the flowers tested. The familiar plant names in the top ten regularly include begonia, calibrachoa, coleus, impatiens, marigold, petunia, verbena, and zinnia.[8]

❦

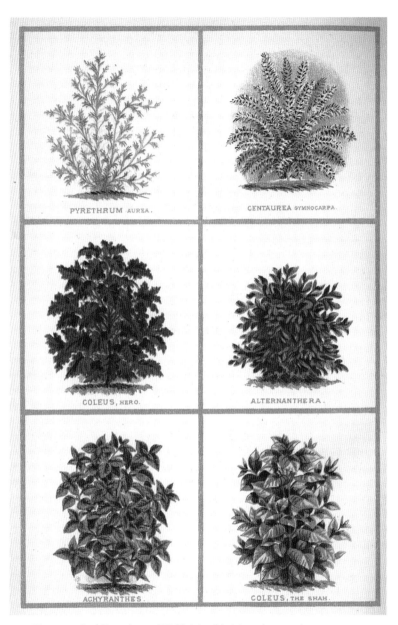

🌿 *Figure 13.1.* Bedding plants. (*Vick's Monthly Magazine,* 1881.)

In the nineteenth century, it made sense for hybridizers to breed new plants from varieties that gardeners were familiar with already. That would make any marketing of the plant that much easier. That argument seems to hold to the present day.

Many of these plants, like the petunia, originally came from South America, Asia, or Africa. It was the South American petunia that became the subject of Vick's hybridizing. The origin was not as important as was the plant's position in the marketplace. Vick chose to hybridize mainly familiar plants. Thus, he continued to put that plant in front of the customer as an important element of the garden. And, of course, that is what he listed and wrote about in his catalog and magazine.

The Victorian period set the standard for what to plant in the home garden. The seed companies and nurseries have done a great job in selling us the same plants for the past hundred and fifty years. At a recent trade show for the green industry, a nurseryman said, "Breeders go where the money is."

Vick's catalogs and magazine contributed to gardening culture, but a particular kind of culture, one that valued flower gardening. Flowers became important in that Victorian setting in part because flower seed merchants like Vick wrote about their essential role for every home, especially that of the worker and middle class. The seedsmen and plantsmen of the period were also drawing from the culture's view of women and the garden. They fostered a Victorian sentimentality about the value of flowers for a popular audience eager and ready to hear their message and put it into practice both in the garden and in the house.

Today every garden center sells several varieties of coleus, a plant that adds color to any garden. The coleus was also an essential plant for the Victorian garden (fig. 13.2). Vick wrote, "The Coleus for bedding is more used than any other plant, and the varieties of it are almost innumerable. Every spring many new ones are offered which have been originated from seed, and they present some wonderful combinations of colors."[9]

Figure 13.2. Coleus. (*Vick's Monthly Magazine*, 1880.)

The annuals from the nineteenth century continue as an important choice for the home gardener. A reader wrote to Vick in 1878, "The pansy is my favorite flower, they are almost human" (fig. 13.3).[10] To this day, pansies remain a top-selling annual for the home garden.

I once visited the beautiful Irish garden and estate Powerscourt, outside Dublin, which dates back to the seventeenth century. The perennial bed in the garden includes 750 different varieties, planted along two borders, with a walkway in the center—truly an outstanding example of its type.

On my way to the parking lot for the car, I thought I would stop in the open greenhouse and gift shop. Outside the greenhouse was a small cart with three levels filled with pansies for sale. This was late October, and there was certainly time to still plant pansies, which can take a bit of cold. Then I thought how this flower, the pansy, is quite popular here in the US. It is a big seller in garden centers, especially in the spring, but also in early fall.

❧

By the 1840s, the verbena was the most popular bedding annual. It remained in that position into the twentieth century.[11] It is still available in new varieties today and has become a top-seller with Proven Winners. Vick wrote, "Among our garden flowers none is more valuable and none more highly prized than the Verbena. . . . We know of nothing that will make a finer bed."[12]

Gardeners might say that they like to try something new in the garden, but even the newer plant has to relate to a variety the gardener knows something about already. Gardeners want a plant that has already performed well in the garden. Thus, Vick sold the same plant seeds in every catalog, on occasion offering a newer variety of the same familiar plant. It is thus no surprise that we see pansies, petunias, marigolds, and alyssum sold around the world. These familiar, old-fashioned plants have held up over time. They still are able to make money for the garden industry.

James Vick sold annuals that he loved. His customers often expressed their satisfaction with his plant seeds. The flowers bloomed in the gardens of Vick's customers and their gardens became the envy of the neighborhood, as many faithful buyers mentioned in their letters to Vick.

Figure 13.3. Pansies. (*Vick's Monthly Magazine,* 1881.)

Vick's purpose in starting his company was to spread the love of flowers among his customers. His customers would in turn echo his words like
a gardener from California who wrote, "No other florist has done as much
as you to create a love of flowers . . . If you were going to run for office, and
we could vote, you would find yourself a popular candidate."[13] In the process, Vick sold the same Victorian flowers that continue to be popular in
gardens today.

Conclusion

F or more than the twenty years that James Vick managed his company, he devoted himself to spreading the love of flowers. He once wrote, "How we do admire the true, hearty love of flowers, with no sham, no straining for effect, no anxiety about what people will think, no ostentation, but a genuine, whole-souled love of the beautiful creations of Infinite Goodness and Wisdom."[1]

The story of James Vick's success centers on his bond to the many gardeners who sought advice from him, read his catalog and magazine, and bought his seeds.

The several methods Vick used to build a relationship with his customers reflect his deep sense of ethics at a time when businesses were free to entice customers in any way they chose. When he spoke of his desire to spread the love of flowers, his passion convinced his readers of his honest intentions at a time when many businesses sought "hype" over integrity. Phineas T. Barnum became a voice for such a crass view of promotion. "Anything to get one's name in the paper" became his credo.

At the same time, the country was entering an era in which multiple means to promote a company or product became available. Department stores like Wanamaker used many methods to entice customers, mostly women, to enter the store and purchase items he provided. Wanamaker's publicity methods included decorated store windows, billboards, special teas held in the store, and newspaper advertising.

Vick issued his first seed catalog in 1861, the same year that John Wanamaker opened his first store in Philadelphia. The methods Vick used to build a relationship with his customers represented his own early version of what we now recognize as an integrated marketing approach, necessary for any successful business.

First and foremost, Vick had an abiding respect for the role of the media as an educator. He wrote, "We know and acknowledge the influence of the press. We want that influence always on the side of right. The press is one of the greatest educators in this land, and we want the people to receive a good education."[2] He followed up on that appreciation of the role of newspapers and magazines by often sending editors copies of his catalog as well as a few seed packets.

The editor of a paper from Massachusetts wrote in 1867, "James Vick . . . has done more to secure choice seed, and import rare bulbs and plants, than any other person in the United States. His being an editor and publisher for a score of years, where man's courage, patience and temper is so tried, even purses made to suffer, by slack subscribers and tardy pay-masters, has not one whit lessened his ideas of beauty, but he has for the past six years been using the pen, shovel, hoe, and exquisite taste, in the floral department; so no one need remain ignorant of method, or destitute of seeds and bulbs for flower gardens, if they but apply in season to him for supplies."[3]

Another newspaper editor from Arkansas said, "We were surprised, but greatly pleased to receive, a few days since, the first number of your very beautiful 'Floral Guide' for 1876. It seems that you never forget your friends. What with your excellent 'Quarterlies,' and the nice plants and flowers that we have grown from seeds received from you, we shall have abundant occasion to remember you in turn."[4]

Enlisting the counsel of the J. Walter Thompson ad agency, Vick's advertising appeared in major magazines and newspapers around the country. The ad was usually a simple rectangular or square black-and-white block of information about the company with an invitation to write in for a catalog.

Vick spent as much as $100,000 a year on advertising with Thompson. When Vick died, his sons unfortunately discontinued the contract. James

Vick Jr. thought he had enough business and no longer wanted to advertise. Thompson said, "Vick, you are crazy; it will only be a question of time until you are bankrupt."[5] Nurseryman J. Elliott Wilkinson, a personal friend of Thompson, recalled that only a few years after this, Vick's daughter had to seek work as a governess for one of Wilkinson's Pittsburgh friends.

We would know less about Vick had he not published many of the letters he received from his readers. His readers often asked him to publish their letters so others could learn from their garden experience, whether it was a success or not. Children often wrote him with questions about the garden and flowers.

Another form of reaching his customers was to offer them framed chromolithographs of flowers that he sold. The colored illustrations, measuring nineteen by twenty-four inches in size, often included at the bottom, in tiny print, the name of each of the flowers. Vick wrote, "They are made from paintings of flowers, taken from our own grounds."[6]

State fairs gave Vick a chance to see the country and promote his seed company. He traveled to a few of them and sometimes won awards for displays of his flowers. He also encouraged his customers to enter flowers from their own garden, rewarding them if they received special honors at any fair.

To give his customers a chance to see his own work, Vick cultivated fields of flowers both at his home and his seed farm for customers to visit. Such visits often became the subject of newspaper articles. In 1870 the agricultural weekly *Moore's Rural New Yorker* wrote, "Here the visitor who loves the beautiful in nature will always find the gates open and some one to point out and explain the history and value of the many rarities that, in season and out of season, embellish the grounds."[7]

In towns and cities around the country, Vick encouraged local seed clubs. In such groups one customer would enlist others in the neighborhood to buy seeds as part of a joint order. The goal was lofty—to make a beautiful neighborhood. Vick wrote, "One or two in any place, by a little exertion, can persuade many who never before cultivated a flower, to allow a few papers [seed packets] to be ordered for them."[8]

In his choice of methods to promote his company, Vick illustrated skill both in building up his list of customers and keeping his name in the public eye. The fact that he controlled much of this interaction with his customers contributed to making him one of the most successful seed merchants in the nineteenth century.

Vick once gave a talk about his business to an evening class at the Rochester Business University. The local paper covered the talk and reported that "Mr. Vick illustrated the necessity for honest purposes, conscientious practice, persistent and skillfully directed labor, and, liberality in all business dealings, as essentials to success. He exhorted all to elevate their self-respect as the only fit beacon in life."[9]

Today we might refer to Vick's promotional methods as an early example of integrated marketing communication, with four discernible methods to build a relationship with a customer.[10] First, he employed *paid* communication, like advertising. Then there was *earned* communication, which meant newspapers and magazines writing articles about him and his business. Third, Vick's program of developing seed clubs around the country showed an example of *shared* communication, a method of reaching his audience through emphasizing the influence one person can have on another. Finally, his publications, especially the catalog and magazine, provide a powerful example of *owned* communication.

In the early years of his seed business, *Moore's Rural New Yorker* published more than a column's length of glowing tribute to Vick. By then he owned a seed house in downtown Rochester and published annual catalogs. The editor wrote, "If any think the above [tribute to Vick] a simple 'puff' or paid for solicited notice, they are mistaken. It is entirely voluntary, without hint or solicitation from Mr. Vick,—given because we believe the man and his establishment worthy of being commended to the tens of thousands of our readers who cultivate or admire the most beautiful of earth's products—Flowers."[11]

Postscript

ames Vick died in Rochester on May 16, 1882.

In 1883, John S. Harris, the president of the Minnesota State Horticultural Society, mentioned both Charles Darwin and James Vick in his annual address to the members. Harris said, "I have to record the names of two men, whose labors have been largely for the benefit of farmers and horticulturists, Charles Darwin and James Vick.

"Charles Darwin, who died at the ripe age of seventy-four, was considered the greatest horticulturist of the age. He was the author of many valuable works . . .

"James Vick, who died at Rochester, N.Y. May 16, was aged 64 years. Although English by birth, he was truly an American horticulturist, and his name had become a household word, through his genial quality and his devotion to horticulture in all its departments. At the time of his death he was at the head of one of the largest seed establishments in America, and his Floral Guide had a circulation of over 200,000. His success has been marvelous. His labors are finished, but the good he has done will endure forever."[1]

Notes

Foreword

1. Schuyler, "Andrew Jackson Downing," 96.
2. *Manufacturer and Builder* 1, no. 5 (January 1869): 150.
3. *Manufacturer and Builder* 16, no. 2 (February 1884): 47.
4. *Manufacturer and Builder* 26, no. 1 (February 1894): 23.
5. Bailey, *Standard Cyclopedia of Horticulture*, 1601.

Introduction

1. *Vick's Illustrated Monthly* (June 1879): 182.
2. Adams, *Restoring American Gardens*, 54.
3. *Vick's Illustrated Monthly* (May 1881): 136.
4. Blakeman, *Integrated Marketing Communication*, 20.
5. Blakeman, 21.

Chapter 1: Vick the Writer

1. Shapiro, "James Vick: The Friendly Seedsman," 2–3.
2. *Genesee Farmer* (January 1, 1831): 1.
3. "Editor's Table," *Genesee Farmer* (January 1855): 34.
4. *Rural Annual and Horticultural Directory*, 80.
5. Parks, "The Cultivation of Flower City," 40.
6. *Vick's Illustrated Catalogue and Floral Guide*, 1868, 3.
7. *Eagle County Press* (Polo, IL), April 20, 1867.
8. *Rural Annual and Horticultural Directory*, 81.
9. *Rural Annual and Horticultural Directory*, 81.
10. *Vick's Illustrated Catalogue and Floral Guide*, 1872, contents page.
11. *Vick's Illustrated Floral Guide*, 1873, 149.
12. *Vick's Illustrated Catalogue and Floral Guide*, 1878, 1.
13. *Vick's Illustrated Monthly* (January 1878): 1.

14. "Persons Who Have Improved the Country: James Vick," xxxiii.

15. *Vick's Illustrated Monthly* (August 1878): 235.

16. *Vick's Illustrated Monthly* (February 1879): 38.

17. *Vick's Illustrated Monthly* (May 1878): 151.

18. *Vick's Illustrated Monthly* (March 1878): 92.

19. *Vick's Illustrated Monthly* (May 1878): 140.

20. *Vick's Illustrated Monthly* (January 1878): 19.

Chapter 2: Flowers in the Garden

1. Hunt and Willis, *The Genius of the Place,* 198.

2. Langley, quoted in Hunt and Willis, 182, 185.

3. Woodbridge, *The Stourhead Landscape,* 46.

4. Thorburn, *Catalogue of Kitchen Garden,* 16.

5. Richardson, *The Arcadian Friends,* 144.

6. Shenstone, "Unconnected Thoughts on Gardening," 289.

7. Knox, "On the Pleasures of a Garden," 332.

8. See Crane, *Flowers from Shakespeare's Garden.*

9. Scourse, *The Victorians and Their Flowers,* 37.

10. Romie Stott, "How Flower-Obsessed Victorians Encoded Messages in Bouquets," Atlas Obscura, August 15, 2016, https://www.atlasobscura.com/articles/how-flowerobsessed-victorians-encoded-messages-in-bouquets.

11. Arnold Arboretum website, posts on "plant collecting," https://www.arboretum.harvard.edu/tag/plant-collecting.

12. Vick, *Vick's Flower and Vegetable Garden,* 145.

13. Kingsbury, *Hybrid,* 158.

14. *Vick's Illustrated Monthly* (December 1878): 367.

15. *Gardening Illustrated* 5, no. 220 (May 26, 1883): 143.

16. *The Garden: An Illustrated Weekly Journal of Gardening in All Its Branches* 20, no. 519 (October 29, 1881): 439.

17. Kingsbury, *Hybrid,* 147.

18. *Vick's Illustrated Monthly* (August 1878): 240.

19. *Vick's Illustrated Monthly* (July 1878): 213.

20. *Vick's Illustrated Catalogue and Floral Guide,* 1868, iv.

Chapter 3: The Garden Industry in the Nineteenth Century

1. Wilder, "The Horticulture of Boston and Vicinity," 625.

2. Seaburg and Paterson, *Merchant Prince of Boston.*

3. Lockwood, *Gardens of Colony and State,* 44.

4. Scourse, *The Victorians and Their Flowers,* 13.

5. Cary, *Memoir of Thomas Handasyd Perkins,* 243.

6. Wilder, "The Horticulture of Boston and Vicinity," 625.

7. Stuart, *The Plants That Shaped Our Gardens,* 69.

8. Hunnewell, *Life, Letters, and Diary of Horatio Hollis Hunnewell,* 52.

9. "Seasonable Hints," *Gardeners' Monthly and Horticulturist* 18, no. 212 (August 1876): 225.

10. Lambert, Buckler, and Meehan, *The Art of Gardening,* 13.

11. Rawson, *Eden on the Charles,* 177.

12. Pregill and Volkman, *Landscapes in History,* 555.

13. Pregill and Volkman, 556.

14. Downing, *A Treatise on the Theory and Practice of Landscape Gardening,* 20.

15. Bowditch, *A Descriptive Catalogue of Flower-Seeds for Sale,* 3.

16. Edward L. Koethens, "Horticulture in Pittsburgh," *Gardeners' Monthly and Horti-culturist* 23, no. 270 (June 1881): 167.

17. Tice, *Gardening in America,* 37.

18. "Vick's Illustrated Floral Guide," *Gardeners' Monthly and Horticulturist* 15, no. 1 (January 1873): 27–28.

19. *Attractive Home Grounds,* 2.

20. "Beautiful Rural Homes," *Vick's Illustrated Monthly* (June 1881): 162.

21. J. H. Hale, "The Nursery Business," *Florist's Exchange* 7, no. 17 (March 30, 1895): 402.

22. R. & J. Farquhar Company, *Gardening in a Nutshell.*

23. *Buist's Almanac and Garden Manual,* 132.

24. *Vick's Illustrated Monthly* (February 1878): 63.

25. Carmichael, *Putting Down Roots,* 63.

26. *Vick's Illustrated Monthly* (May 1878): 129.

27. *Vick's Illustrated Monthly* (July 1878): 201.

28. *Vick's Illustrated Monthly* (May 1878): 147.

29. *Vick's Illustrated Monthly* (August 1878): 251.

30. "An Immense Seed Establishment," *Horticulturist* 22 (October 1867): 320.

31. Weishan and Roig, *From a Victorian Garden,* 25.

32. *Vick's Illustrated Monthly* (October 1880): 322.

33. Newcomb, *Popular Annuals of Eastern North America,* 19.

Chapter 4: Women and Flowers

1. Repton, excerpts from the "Red Book" for Blaise Castle.

2. Johnson, *Every Woman Her Own Flower Gardener,* 8.

3. Seaton, "Gardening Books for the Commuter's Wife," 45.

4. Seaton, 47.

5. Taylor, *The Victorian Flower Garden,* 155–56.

6. Stuart, *The Plants That Shaped Our Gardens,* 68.

7. Elliott, *Victorian Gardens,* 210.

8. Scourse, *The Victorians and Their Flowers,* 177.

9. Scourse, 172.

10. Johnson, *Every Lady Her Own Flower Gardener*, 11.

11. "The Preservation of Wild Flowers," *Godey's Lady's Book* 23, no. 1 (July 1841): 23–24.

12. Ingram, "Victorian Flower Power."

13. Turner, *The Garden Diary of Martha Turnbull*.

14. *Vick's Illustrated Monthly* (March 1878): 77.

15. *Vick's Illustrated Monthly* (April 1878): 116.

16. *Vick's Illustrated Monthly* (April 1878): 117.

Chapter 5: Flower Garden Fashion

1. Breck, *The Flower Garden*, 18.

2. Breck, 19.

3. Breck, 22.

4. Breck, 26–27.

5. Henderson, *Gardening for Pleasure*, 30.

6. Henderson, 35.

7. *American Agriculturist* 47, no. 3 (March 1888): 91.

8. Hill, *Grandmother's Garden*, 60.

9. *Vick's Illustrated Monthly* (January 1879): 12.

Chapter 6: The Vick Seed Company

1. *Vick's Illustrated Monthly* (February 1880): 33.

2. McKelvey, *Rochester: The Flower City*, 13.

3. *Vick's Floral Guide*, 1874, 23.

4. *Vick's Floral Guide*, 1874, 25.

5. *Vick's Floral Guide*, 1880, inside front cover.

6. Van Ravenswaay, *A Nineteenth-Century Garden*, 21.

7. *Gardeners' Monthly and Horticulturist* 22, no. 255 (March 1880): 91.

8. "Vick, James," in Garraty and Carnes, *American National Biography*.

9. *Vick's Illustrated Catalogue and Floral Guide*, 1868, back cover.

10. "Vick, James," in *National Cyclopaedia of American Biography*, 4:469.

11. *Vick's Illustrated Monthly* (February 1879): 40.

12. *Vick's Illustrated Monthly* (May 1878): 149.

13. Scourse, *The Victorians and Their Flowers*, 6.

14. *Vick's Illustrated Monthly* (November 1878): 340.

15. Rowell, *The Men Who Advertise*, 140.

16. *Vick's Floral Guide*, 1877, 138.

17. McKelvey, *Rochester: The Flower City*, 234.

18. *Vick's Illustrated Monthly* (May 1879): 154.

19. *Vick's Illustrated Catalogue and Floral Guide,* 1866, i.
20. *Vick's Illustrated Monthly* (February 1880): 33.
21. Nichols, *English Pleasure Gardens,* 293.
22. *Vick's Illustrated Monthly* (February 1878): 33.

Chapter 7: The Garden Catalog

1. *Vick's Illustrated Monthly* (June 1878): 178.
2. Leopold, *The Victorian Garden,* 142.
3. *Vick's Illustrated Catalogue of Hardy Bulbs and Floral Guide,* 1866.
4. *Vick's Illustrated Catalogue and Floral Guide,* 1868, ii.
5. *Vick's Illustrated Catalogue and Floral Guide,* 1871, 1.
6. *Vick's Illustrated Catalogue and Floral Guide,* 1871, 1.
7. *Vick's Illustrated Catalogue and Floral Guide,* 1868, 2.
8. *Vick's Illustrated Catalogue and Floral Guide,* 1871, 1.
9. *Vick's Illustrated Catalogue and Floral Guide,* 1872, 2.
10. *Vick's Illustrated Catalogue and Floral Guide,* 1872, 1.
11. *Vick's Illustrated Catalogue and Floral Guide,* 1880, 1.
12. *Vick's Illustrated Catalogue and Floral Guide,* 1874, 1.
13. *Vick's Illustrated Catalogue and Floral Guide,* 1874, 177.
14. *The Garden: An Illustrated Weekly Journal of Gardening in All Its Branches* (January 28, 1882): 64.
15. *Vick's Illustrated Catalogue and Floral Guide,* 1878, 1.
16. McKelvey, *Rochester: The Flower City,* 13.

Chapter 8: Promoting the Seed Business

1. *Vick's Illustrated Monthly* (November 1879): 327.
2. *Vick's Illustrated Monthly* (September 1878): 277.
3. *Vick's Illustrated Catalogue and Floral Guide,* 1868, iii.
4. Hyams, *English Cottage Gardens,* 156.
5. Davies, *The Victorian Flower Garden,* 23.
6. *Vick's Illustrated Floral Guide,* 1873, 22.
7. *Journal of the New York State Agricultural Society* (1873), 88.
8. *Vick's Illustrated Monthly* (November 1879): 331.
9. *Vick's Illustrated Monthly* (June 1878): 192.
10. *Vick's Illustrated Monthly* (December 1879): 376.
11. *Vick's Floral Guide,* 1880, 8.
12. *Vick's Illustrated Monthly* (April 1878): 117.
13. Quoted in Parks, "The Cultivation of Flower City," 39.
14. *Vick's Illustrated Monthly* (February 1878): 65.

15. *American Agriculturist* 38 (1879): 516.

16. Parks, "The Cultivation of Flower City," 40.

17. *N. W. Ayer & Son's Newspaper Annual,* 518.

18. *Moore's Rural New Yorker* (November 2, 1867): 351.

19. *Vick's Illustrated Catalogue and Floral Guide,* 1870, 1.

20. *Vick's Illustrated Monthly* (March 1878): 94.

21. *Vick's Illustrated Monthly* (May 1878): 142.

22. *Vick's Illustrated Monthly* (November 1878): 332.

23. *Gardeners' Monthly and Horticulturist* 24, no. 280 (April 1882): 125.

24. *Vick's Illustrated Monthly* (November 1878): 327–28.

25. *Vick's Illustrated Monthly* (February 1880): 46.

26. *Vick's Illustrated Monthly* (June 1879): 183.

27. *Rural Annual and Horticultural Directory,* 82.

28. *Vick's Illustrated Monthly* (February 1878): 61.

29. *Gardeners' Monthly and Horticulturist* 24, no. 282 (June 1882): 188.

30. *Letters of Celia Thaxter,* 133.

31. Norcross, "Cataloging America's Cultural Roots," 19.

32. McKelvey, *Rochester: The Flower City,* 234.

Chapter 9: Building His Business

1. "Vick, James," in Garraty and Carnes, *American National Biography,* 348.

2. McIntosh, *History of Monroe County,* 113.

3. *Vick's Illustrated Catalogue and Floral Guide,* 1871, 3.

4. *Vick's Floral Guide,* 1881, 1.

5. Harkness and Olney, "John Walton (1834–1914): Artist," 177.

6. *Vick's Floral Guide,* 1881, 1.

7. Allingham, "The Technologies of Nineteenth-Century Illustration."

8. *Vick's Illustrated Monthly* (September 1880): 296.

9. *Vick's Illustrated Catalogue and Floral Guide,* 1870, 1.

10. Beckwith, "Early Botanists of Rochester and Vicinity," 46–48.

11. *Vick's Illustrated Floral Guide,* 1873, 4.

12. *Vick's Illustrated Floral Guide,* 1873, 2.

13. *Vick's Illustrated Monthly* (February 1878): 33.

Chapter 10: Vick Lays Out the Flower Garden

1. *Vick's Illustrated Catalogue and Floral Guide,* 1868, 2–3; emphases in original.

2. *Vick's Illustrated Monthly* (October 1879): 292.

3. *Vick's Illustrated Monthly* (October 1879): 293.

4. *Vick's Illustrated Monthly* (September 1880): 291.

5. *Gardeners' Monthly and Horticulturist* 27, no. 324 (December 1885): 375.

6. Downing, *A Treatise on the Theory and Practice of Landscape Gardening*, 357.

7. *Vick's Illustrated Monthly* (July 1879): 195.

8. Long, *Ornamental Gardening for Americans*, 206–7.

9. Simonds, *Landscape-Gardening*, 150.

10. *Vick's Illustrated Monthly* (February 1880): 34.

11. *Vick's Illustrated Monthly* (February 1880): 35.

12. Vick, *Vick's Flower and Vegetable Garden*, 17.

13. Vick, 17.

14. *Vick's Illustrated Monthly* (February 1880): 34.

15. Beecher and Stowe, *The American Woman's Home*, 382.

16. *Vick's Floral Guide*, 1882, 3–4.

17. *Vick's Floral Guide*, 1874, 3, inside back cover.

18. *Currie's Monthly* 2, no. 7 (July 1886): 3.

19. Vick, *Vick's Flower and Vegetable Garden*, 18.

20. *Vick's Floral Guide*, 1874, 13.

21. Stuart, *The Garden Triumphant*, 87.

22. Stuart, 87.

23. *Vick's Illustrated Monthly* (February 1879): 39.

24. "Arranging Cut Flowers—Secrets of a Top London Florist," The English Garden, September 4, 2014, https://www.theenglishgarden.co.uk/top-picks/inspiration/arranging _cut_flowers_secrets_of_a_top_london_florist_1_3757385.

25. *Vick's Illustrated Monthly* (August 1878): 225.

26. *Vick's Illustrated Monthly* (September 1880): 298.

Chapter 11: Vick Sells the Same Flowers Year after Year

1. Kingsbury, *Hybrid*, 349.

2. *Vick's Seed Catalog*, 1870, 3.

3. William Robinson, "Petunias," *The Garden: An Illustrated Weekly Journal of Gardening in All Its Branches* (August 29, 1891): 195.

4. *Vick's Illustrated Monthly* (May 1879): 133.

5. Bailey, *Cyclopedia of American Horticulture*, s.v. "petunia," 2564.

6. "Petunia History," Esbenshades Garden Centers, https://www.esbenshades.com /jzv/inf/ABriefHistoryOfThePetunia.

7. Kingsbury, *Hybrid*, 4, 6.

8. *Vick's Illustrated Monthly* (May 1878): 147.

9. *Vick's Illustrated Monthly* (June 1879): 170–71.

10. *Vick's Illustrated Monthly* (January 1878): 29.

11. Kingsbury, *Hybrid*, 349.

12. Newcomb, *Popular Annuals of Eastern North America,* 77.

13. *Vick's Illustrated Monthly* (August 1882): 231.

Chapter 12: Victorian Flowers That Vick Loved

1. The same flowers appeared in 1896 in Mathews, "The Beautifying of Public and Private Grounds." More recently, Katherine Knight Rusk presents a similar list of annuals for creating a Victorian-style garden in *Renovating the Victorian House,* 160.

Chapter 13: Vick's Success

1. Goody, *The Culture of Flowers,* 70.

2. Jashemski, "'The Garden of Hercules at Pompeii.'"

3. Goody, *The Culture of Flowers,* 124.

4. Hyams, *English Cottage Gardens,* 21.

5. Hyams, 27.

6. Hyams, 197.

7. "Top 50 Best Selling Annuals," Proven Winners, https://www.provenwinners.com/professionals/top-50.

8 ."Annual Flower Research: Results," West Central Research and Outreach Center, https://wcroc.cfans.umn.edu/flower-research-results.

9. *Vick's Illustrated Monthly* (November 1881): 348.

10. *Vick's Illustrated Monthly* (February 1878): 62.

11. Gorer, *The Growth of Gardens,* 145.

12. *Vick's Illustrated Monthly* (January 1878): 5.

13. *Vick's Illustrated Monthly* (April 1878): 116.

Conclusion

1. *Vick's Floral Guide,* 1876, 62.

2. *Vick's Floral Guide,* 1876, 56.

3. *Vick's Illustrated Catalogue and Floral Guide,* 1868, inside front cover.

4. *Vick's Floral Guide,* 1876, 56.

5. Elliott, *Adventures of a Horticulturist,* 115.

6. *Vick's Illustrated Catalogue and Floral Guide,* 1878, inside front cover.

7. "Industrial Men: Popular Seedsmen," *Moore's Rural New Yorker* 21, no. 7 (February 12, 1870): 105.

8. *Vick's Illustrated Catalogue and Floral Guide,* 1878, 3.

9. "An Enjoyable and Profitable Affair," *Rochester Union Advertiser,* December 15, 1876, 3.

10. Luttrell and Capizzo, *Public Relations Campaigns,* 40.
11. *Moore's Rural New Yorker,* November 2, 1867, 351.

Postscript

1. Harris, "President's Annual Address," 52.

Bibliography

Periodicals

American Agriculturist
Currie's Monthly
Eagle County Press (Polo, IL)
Florist's Exchange
The Garden: An Illustrated Weekly Journal of Gardening in All Its Branches
Gardeners' Monthly and Horticulturist
Gardening Illustrated
Genesee Farmer
Godey's Lady's Book
Horticulturist
Journal of the New York State Agricultural Society
Manufacturer and Builder
Moore's Rural New Yorker
Rochester Union Advertiser
Rural Annual and Horticultural Directory
Vick's Floral Guide
Vick's Illustrated Catalogue and Floral Guide
Vick's Illustrated Catalogue of Hardy Bulbs and Floral Guide
Vick's Illustrated Floral Guide
Vick's Illustrated Monthly
Vick's Illustrated Monthly Magazine
Vick's Magazine
Vick's Monthly Magazine
Vick's Seed Catalog

Other Sources

Adams, Denise Wiles. *Restoring American Gardens: An Encyclopedia of Heirloom Ornamental Plants, 1640–1940*. Portland, OR: Timber, 2004.

Allingham, Philip. "The Technologies of Nineteenth-Century Illustration: Woodblock Engraving, Steel Engraving, and Other Processes." Victorian Web. Last modified July 11, 2017. http://www.victorianweb.org/art/illustration/tech1.html.

Attractive Home Grounds. New Haven, CT: Elm City Nursery, 1894.

Bailey, Liberty H., ed. *Cyclopedia of American Horticulture.* 4 vols. New York: Macmillan, 1900–1902.

———, ed. *Standard Cyclopedia of Horticulture.* New edition. Vol. 3. New York: Macmillan, 1928.

Beckwith, Florence. "Early Botanists of Rochester and Vicinity and the Botanical Section." *Proceedings of the Rochester Academy of Science* 5 (February 1912): 39–58.

Beecher, Catherine Esther, and Harriet Beecher Stowe. *The American Woman's Home, or Principles of Domestic Science.* New York: J. B. Ford, 1869.

Blakeman, Robyn. *Integrated Marketing Communication.* 2nd ed. Lanham, MD: Rowman and Littlefield, 2015.

Bowditch, Azell. *A Descriptive Catalogue of Flower-Seeds for Sale by Azell Bowditch at the Massachusetts Horticultural Seed & Fruit Store, School Street, Boston.* Boston: Azell Bowditch, 1854.

Breck, Joseph. *The Flower Garden, or Breck's Book of Flowers.* Rev. and enlarged ed. Boston: John P. Jewett, 1856.

Buist's Almanac and Garden Manual. Philadelphia: Robert Buist Jr., 1872.

Carmichael, Marcia C. *Putting Down Roots: Gardening Insights from Wisconsin's Early Settlers.* Madison: Wisconsin Historical Society Press, 2011.

Cary, Thomas G. *Memoir of Thomas Handasyd Perkins.* Boston: Little, Brown, 1856.

Crane, Walter. *Flowers from Shakespeare's Garden: A Posy from the Plays.* Self-published, CreateSpace, 2016.

Davies, Jennifer. *The Victorian Flower Garden.* London: BBC Books, 1991.

Downing, Andrew Jackson. *A Treatise on the Theory and Practice of Landscape Gardening, Adapted to North America.* New York: Wiley and Putnam, 1841.

Elliott, Brent. *Victorian Gardens.* Portland, OR: Timber, 1986.

Elliott, J. Wilkinson. *Adventures of a Horticulturist.* Point Loma, CA: printed by the author, 1935.

Goody, Jack. *The Culture of Flowers.* New York: Cambridge University Press, 1993.

Gorer, Richard. *The Growth of Gardens.* London: Faber and Faber, 1978.

Harkness, Bernard E., and Mabel G. Olney. "John Walton (1834–1914): Artist." *Huntia* 2 (October 1965): 171–79.

Harris, John S. "President's Annual Address." *Annual Report of the Minnesota State Horticultural Society.* Minneapolis: Johnson, Smith, and Harrison, 1883.

Henderson, Peter. *Gardening for Pleasure: A Guide to the Amateur in the Fruit, Vegetable, and Flower Garden.* New York: Orange Judd, 1875.

Hill, May Brawley. *Grandmother's Garden: The Old-Fashioned American Garden, 1865–1915.* New York: Harry N. Abrams, 1995.

Hunnewell, Hollis Horatio. *Life, Letters, and Diary of Horatio Hollis Hunnewell.* Vol. 2. Boston: printed by the author, 1906.

Hunt, John Dixon, and Peter Willis, eds. *The Genius of the Place: The English Landscape Garden, 1620–1820.* Cambridge, MA: MIT Press, 1988.

Hyams, Edward. *English Cottage Gardens*. London: Nelson, 1970.

Ingram, Annie Merrill. "Victorian Flower Power." http://commonplace.online/article/victorian-flower-power.

Jashemski, Wilhelmina F. "'The Garden of Hercules at Pompeii' (II.viii.6): The Discovery of a Commercial Flower Garden." *American Journal of Archaeology* 83, no. 4 (October 1979): 403–11.

Johnson, Louisa. *Every Lady Her Own Flower Gardener: Addressed to the Industrious and Economical*. Rev. and adapted from 14th English ed. New York: C. M. Saxton, 1863.

Johnson, Sophia Orne. *Every Woman Her Own Flower Gardener*. 4th ed. New York: Henry T. Williams, 1874.

Kingsbury, Noel. *Hybrid: The History and Science of Plant Breeding*. Chicago: University of Chicago Press, 2011.

Knox, Vicesimus. "On the Pleasures of a Garden." In *The Genius of the Place*, edited by John Dixon Hunt and Peter Willis, 330–32. Cambridge, MA: MIT Press, 1988.

Lambert, Luna, James R. Buckler, and Kathryn Meehan. *The Art of Gardening: Maryland Landscapes and the American Garden Aesthetic, 1730–1930*. Easton, MD: Historical Society of Talbot County, 1985. Exhibition catalog.

Langley, Batty. *New Principles of Gardening*. London: A. Bettesworth and J. Batley, 1728.

Leopold, Allison Kyle. *The Victorian Garden*. New York: Clarkson Potter, 1995.

Lockwood, Alice G. B., ed. *Gardens of Colony and State*. Vol. 1. New York: Charles Scribner for the Garden Club of America, 1931.

Long, Elias A. *Ornamental Gardening for Americans*. New York: Orange Judd, 1885.

Luttrell, Regina M., and Luke W. Capizzo. *Public Relations Campaigns: An Integrated Approach*. Los Angeles: Sage, 2019.

Lynes, Russell. *The Tastemakers: The Shaping of American Popular Taste*. New York: Dover, 1980.

Mathews, F. Schuyler. "The Beautifying of Public and Private Grounds: IV: The Church Green." *American Gardening* 17, no. 73 (May 16, 1896): 305–6.

McIntosh, W. H. *History of Monroe County, New York*. Philadelphia: Everts, Ensign, and Everts, 1877.

McKelvey, Blake. *Rochester: The Flower City, 1855–1890*. Cambridge, MA: Harvard University Press, 1949.

Newcomb, Peggy Cornett. *Popular Annuals of Eastern North America, 1865–1914*. Washington, DC: Dunbarton Oaks Research Library and Collection, 1985.

Nichols, Rose Standish. *English Pleasure Gardens*. Boston: David Godine, 2003.

Norcross, Marjorie. "Cataloging America's Cultural Roots." *Cornell Plantations* 47, no. 1 (1992): 15–22.

N. W. Ayer & Son's Newspaper Annual. Philadelphia: N. W. Ayer and Son, 1880.

Parks, Dan. "The Cultivation of Flower City." *Rochester History* 45, nos. 3/4 (July/October 1983): 25–47.

"Persons Who Have Improved the Country: James Vick." *Country Life in America* 1, no. 2 (December 1901): xxxii–xxxiii.

Pregill, Philip, and Nancy J. Volkman. *Landscapes in History: Design and Planning in the Eastern and Western Traditions.* 2nd ed. New York: John Wiley, 1999.

Quest-Ritson, Charles. *The English Garden: A Social History.* Boston: David R. Godine, 2004.

R. & J. Farquhar Company. *Gardening in a Nutshell.* Boston: R. & J. Farquhar, 1898.

Rawson, Michael. *Eden on the Charles: The Making of Boston.* Cambridge, MA: Harvard University Press, 2010.

Repton, Humphry. Excerpts from the "Red Book" for Blaise Castle. In *The Genius of the Place,* edited by John Dixon Hunt and Peter Willis, 359–67. Cambridge, MA: MIT Press, 1988.

Richardson, Tim. *The Arcadian Friends: Inventing the English Landscape Garden.* London: Bantam, 2007.

Rowell, George. *The Men Who Advertise.* New York: Nelson Chesman, 1870.

Rural Annual and Horticultural Directory. Rochester, NY: James Vick Jr., 1856.

Rusk, Katherine Knight. *Renovating the Victorian House.* San Francisco: 101 Productions, 1982.

Schuyler, David. "Andrew Jackson Downing." In *Pioneers of American Landscape Design,* edited by Charles A. Birnbaum and Robin Karson, 96–100. New York: McGraw-Hill, 2000.

Scourse, Nicolette. *The Victorians and Their Flowers.* Portland, OR: Timber, 1984.

Seaburg, Carl, and Paterson, Stanley. *Merchant Prince of Boston: Colonel T. H. Perkins, 1764–1854.* Cambridge, MA: Harvard University Press, 1971.

Seaton, Beverly. "Gardening Books for the Commuter's Wife, 1900–1937." *Landscape* 28, no. 2 (1985): 41–47.

Shapiro, Joey. "James Vick: The Friendly Seedsman." Research paper, University of Rochester, December 10, 2008.

Shenstone, William. "Unconnected Thoughts on Gardening." In *The Genius of the Place,* edited by John Dixon Hunt and Peter Willis, 289–97. Cambridge, MA: MIT Press, 1988.

Simonds, Ossian Cole. *Landscape-Gardening.* New York: Macmillan, 1920.

Stuart, David C. *The Garden Triumphant: A Victorian Legacy.* London: Viking, 1988.

———. *The Plants That Shaped Our Gardens.* Cambridge, MA: Harvard University Press, 2002.

Taylor, Geoffrey. *The Victorian Flower Garden.* London: Skeffington, 1952.

Thaxter, Celia. *Letters of Celia Thaxter.* Edited by Annie Adams Fields and Rose Lamb. Boston: Houghton Mifflin, 1895.

Thorburn, George C. *Catalogue of Kitchen Garden, Herb, Flower, Tree, and Grass Seeds.* New York: Printed by George P. Scott, 1838.

Tice, Patricia M. *Gardening in America, 1830–1910.* Rochester, NY: Strong Museum, 1984.

Turner, Suzanne, ed. *The Garden Diary of Martha Turnbull, Mistress of Rosedown Plantation.* Baton Rouge: Louisiana State University Press, 2012.

Van Ravenswaay, Charles. *A Nineteenth-Century Garden.* New York: Main Street, 1977.

Vick, James. *Vick's Flower and Vegetable Garden*. Rochester, NY: Vick Seed Company, 1876.

"Vick, James." In *American National Biography*, edited by John A. Garraty and Mark C. Carnes, 347–48. Oxford: Oxford University Press, 1999.

"Vick, James." In *National Cyclopaedia of American Biography*, 4:469. New York: James T. White, 1897.

Weishan, Michael, and Cristina Roig. *From a Victorian Garden: Creating the Romance of a Bygone Age Right in Your Own Backyard*. New York: Viking Studio, 2004.

Wilder, Marshall Pinckney. "The Horticulture of Boston and Vicinity." In *The Memorial History of Boston*, vol. 4, edited by Justin Winsor, 607–40. Boston: James R. Osgood, 1881.

Woodbridge, Kenneth. *The Stourhead Landscape: Wiltshire*. London: National Trust, 2002.

Index